HUGUES DE MONTALEMBERT

Up until 1978, the author, a French count by birth, was a painter. He travelled extensively working on documentary films such as *I A Dancer* about Rudolph Nureyev and Margot Fonteyn. He took a deep interest in the culture of the countries he visited: the harlem voodoo in West Africa and Indonesian music in Bali.

On May 25th 1978, when returning to his apartment in New York from a Greenwich Village coffee-house, he was met by two intruders who threw caustic solution in his face. At the age of thirty-five he was blinded for life.

Hugues de Montalembert is currently based in Rome although he continues to travel between Europe, America and South East Asia. The French edition of ECLIPSE became a bestseller when it was published in 1982 and the author is currently working on his second book.

Hugues de Montalembert

ECLIPSE

An Autobiography

Translated from the French
by David Noakes

First published in Great Britain in 1986 by Hodder and Stoughton Ltd.

Sceptre edition 1987

Sceptre is an imprint of Hodder and Stoughton Paperbacks, a division of Hodder and Stoughton Ltd.

British Library C.I.P.

Montalembert, Hugues de
  Eclipse: an autobiography
  1. Blind – Rehabilitation
  2. Blindness – Psychological
    aspects
  I. Title
  II. La Lumière assassinée.
    English
362.4'1'0924   HV1598

ISBN 0-340-40779-4

Printed and bound in Great Britain for Hodder and Stoughton Paperbacks, a division of Hodder and Stoughton Ltd., Mill Road, Dunton Green, Sevenoaks, Kent (Editorial Office: 47 Bedford Square, London, WC1B 3DP) by Richard Clay Ltd., Bungay, Suffolk. Photoset by Rowland Phototypesetting Ltd., Bury St Edmunds, Suffolk.

à VALERIE

AUTHOR'S NOTE

All the names of detectives and policemen, medical personnel, employees of the Carlyle, and patients and personnel of the Lighthouse, as well as the following have been changed to protect their privacy: Cynthia, Désirée, Alicia, Dwike, Mrs Simpson, Valushka, Mr Schwartz, Dr George, Rama, Mr Chang, and Enrico.

ACKNOWLEDGMENT

I wish most of all to thank Victoria Waymouth for working with me on the revision and editing of the English version. It is thanks to her unusual authority and sensitivity that the spirit of *Eclipse* has survived translation.

ONE

For the last few weeks I have felt in danger. There have been warning signs which I haven't been able to analyse. I have been living in New York for two years; I feel morally, spiritually worn out. It is spring and tonight, May 25, in spite of a little rain, I am going for a walk in Washington Square. I live in a small house at the end of the narrow cul-de-sac called MacDougal Alley, at number 13 in fact. The street is a historic place; many well-known painters and writers have lived here.

As I arrive home and start to insert my key in the street door, two hands grab me by the shoulders and violently push me inside. The door closes and I hear the voices of black men giving me orders. They are behind me. In my confusion I can't say how many of them there are. There is a knife. They force me to climb the stairs to the living room on the second floor.

There are two of them, both black. One is tall and strong and holds the knife. The other is effeminate, skinny, maybe Jamaican, with an earring. In their rhythmic voices they demand money. I have thirty dollars with me. I put the bills on the table, but they don't even look at them. The strong one presses the knife against my throat, threatens me, and continues to demand the rest of my money. I don't have any more cash. I explain to him that it's all in the bank and I turn my pockets inside out. He swears, presses the knife against me, and orders me to take off my clothes. I undress. I am afraid. I feel very tired.

I know that I will not find the words that might calm things down. I remember other dangerous situations, in Asia, Vietnam, Africa, that I escaped by diffusing hatred through a force which is not within me tonight.

The effeminate one has disappeared. He has gone up to the

studio where I paint, one flight above. He comes back down carrying a radio, which he turns on full blast. He sits down on the sofa, lights up a joint, and hands it to the man with the knife.

By now I am completely naked. The big one shouts insults and makes demands that I hardly understand. He plays with the knife over my body.

The skinny one gets up and disappears to the floor below. I hear sounds of furniture being moved about, drawers being opened. He seems to be in a fit of rage. I discover later that he has emptied all the drawers into the middle of the room. He comes back up. By the way they talk I know they are heavily drugged, probably on speed. I can't remember their words, but they seem to be disappointed. There is no money in this house, no jewelry, no valuable objects.

Holding the tip of the knife against my throat, the big guy begins to hit me on the head, in the ribs. He runs the knife over my body and I'm afraid he'll kill me, castrate me. In his eyes I see sadism, like a kind of madness, an amusement. And suddenly I realise that it's no longer money that interests him; it's me.

The danger is palpable. I know that if I don't do something, I am going to die. For a second, his eyes turn away from me. A few feet off, hanging from the mantelpiece, is a heavy iron poker with a hook at the end. Quickly, I seize it and hit him with it, as hard as I can, but I haven't aimed at his head. There is a fight, confusion; furniture falls; the poker is grabbed out of my hands.

I know I'll find another poker hanging from the fireplace on the ground floor. I run to the stairs, race to the bedroom, and grab it. The knife is behind me. I strike out. He doesn't seem to feel anything. We go round and round a table. I climb the stairs with him behind me. Upstairs, I see the thin one but pay no attention to him. He doesn't count. I could kill him with a single blow. I get to the middle of the room and face my attacker. This time, I am ready to aim at his head. I am ready to kill. We look at each other. I stare into his eyes to anticipate his next move, and it is at that moment that I receive hot liquid full in the face. I fall to the ground.

I have had just enough time to realise that it was the Jamaican who has thrown it at me. I think, foolishly, that it is coffee he has made without my noticing. I scream. Blinded by the burning liquid, I wipe my eyes and feel something sticky on my fingers. Acid. I recognise it from chemistry lessons. I howl at the top of my lungs. Not because of the pain, but because I am terrified.

I'm afraid of the knife, I'm afraid they'll kill me. I howl so loudly that it scares them and I hear them running down the stairs.

I rush into the kitchen and over the sink splash my face with cold water. It burns.

I wash, wash, and wash.

The police, call the police. Get to a hospital as quickly as possible. I direct myself towards where I know there is a telephone. I am moving in an aquarium. Everything is glaucous. I dial zero. I can't remember the police emergency number. I get the operator, a black woman, I can tell from her voice. As calmly as I can, I ask her to call the police right away. I give her my address. She asks, 'Where is that?' I tell her, 'Near Washington Square.' She asks me, 'Where is Washington Square?' I become desperate.

This is too much for her; I feel that perhaps she won't do anything, that she thinks it's all a joke. New York is immense and so many things go on here. She swears to me that she's going to contact the police. I am hardly reassured.

I hang up, go downstairs, and discover the street door has been left open. I am naked. I close the door.

I get under the shower to wash off the acid, which keeps burning my face and which has dripped onto parts of my body.

Again I wash and wash and wash. But it is still there!

Already I see less. My vision is fuzzier, more opaque.

Suddenly, I realise that under the shower I will not hear the police arrive. I get out of the shower and grope for clothes. I can see scarcely anything now. I stumble over the drawers that have been turned upside down in the middle of the room. I put on the first things I find. I can't find my shoes. I go upstairs but still don't find them.

I come back down and open the street door. I hear people walking by and stop them, saying:

'Please! Call the police. I have been attacked. I have acid in my eyes. Call the police, please get the police!'

The footsteps have stopped, but there is no answer.

'Please, I've been mugged. I have acid in my eyes. Please get the police!'

The steps move on. Still there is no answer.

Finally, someone says to me, 'O.K, don't worry, I'll get help.' I close the door. Now I'm sure that the police will arrive. I take some cigarettes from the bedside table, sit down on the stairs facing the door, and wait. Half an hour passes and nothing happens. I go back to my bedroom and manage to dial the number of a painter friend of mine who lives in the neighbourhood. I explain what happened and ask him to call the police. I go back to the stairs and force myself to smoke to stay calm, hoping that this familiar act will help.

When I understood that it was acid, there was a second when the animal in me reacted with such a violence, with such a roar, that at that moment I nearly lost myself in madness. It has taken all my will, all my vital instincts to stop the panic, to reverse the process. From that moment on, I act. I do not think.

No longer am I tired. The sensation of something irrevocable twists my guts. I know that something very serious has happened, but I don't know exactly what and I don't want to think about it.

I sit on these stairs, smoking. I wait. I don't think. The unreality paralyses my brain. There are knocks at the door. The police have arrived at last, along with a painter friend on his bike. I put out the cigarette. Arms grab and pull me. I stumble down the steps. I am still barefoot. They help me into the police car, which starts off immediately. Soon we are at the hospital, in the emergency room.

They make me lie down on a metal table and male nurses begin to douse me with water.

I am naked. They have taken off all my clothes, they have even taken away my gold baptismal chain, which I will never see again; it will be stolen from this emergency room. New York and its scavengers.

The water is ice cold; the acid burns. I howl. I tremble. My body is nothing but a panic-stricken tremor, which knocks against the metal. I am aware that my sight is diminishing, and I cannot make out the people around me. I see only shadows, as if I were plunged into a deep sea. The metal of the table resounds with the panic of my body. I ask:

'Where is the doctor? Tell me if it's serious. I want to know. Is it serious? I am a painter, I have to know.'

A voice answers me:

'It is very serious.'

I stay on that table a long time. Around me, in the emergency room, there are all kinds of confusion. People groaning, children crying. Someone keeps on bathing my face.

Then I am moved to a brightly lit room. I am put in a metal chair, under a shower, and asked to open my eyes as much as possible and to hold my eyelids open with my fingers. I raise my face towards the shower head, which is covering me with cold water. I am frozen.

There is a nurse. I can make out her silhouette; she is very fat. I stay there, under the shower, for perhaps an hour. My recollections of what follows are confused and vague.

I find myself lying in bed in a room where, all night long, a very gentle nurse bathes my eyes every half hour. I can no longer see anything. I am not in pain and my brain continues to anaesthetise itself. I do not think. Morning comes.

All seems so irrevocable.

TWO

As I said, there had been warning signs.

'In life you must listen to your instinct, then do exactly the opposite,' I was told one day by a Pole who had escaped from the death camps.

Yet recognising the fact that we mustn't let the animal in us dominate the man, I regret not having followed my premonitions more instinctively.

Several months before the attack, at a turning point in my life and sensing vagueness in my future, I asked Dwike, a Voodoo priest, to do a divination for me.

I went to Harlem, to a basement on 114th Street, near Lexington Avenue. Dwike said some prayers to Legba, one of the most powerful Voodoos, then to Fa, the Voodoo of divination. He used the Yoruba language with a strong American accent. He took out of a bag a glistening shell, as long as a finger, and a small black stone.

I shook these objects together, then separated them, one in each hand. His interpretation would differ according to whether the hand he pointed to held the stone or the shell.

'You have strong vitality, my boy, but what a waste, a waste of time, a waste of energy! You can work hard with no results. You work for nothing! There are in you two guys. You don't fit in your family. You are some kind of gypsy. You don't believe either in rules or in social rank. Still, you have got your father inside, but you are not on the same side of the door. Don't fight the conventional side; you are conservative also. But there is something different in you that propels you into the future. You belong to the twenty-first century. You can't be both; you can't be a hippie in a Brooks Brothers suit.

'You have decided to attach more importance to the mind than to the body. You are wrong! You must change, or else you risk thrombosis.

'You had an argument, recently, with someone very close to you.'

He threw the shell down.

'Your wife is like the ocean, always restless, always under pressure. A lot of fights and still there is something very strong between you.

'Whatever you want to do in life, no problem! Your brain works well, just put your mind into your body. Don't think you are a superman; that can only cause the ruin of your body.

'Have you ever worked with your hands? Sculpture? Painting? Well then, it must be strong painting, done more with your fingers than with a brush.

'Now what about women, my boy?

'Sometimes for you it's full moon. But be careful; sometimes there is a halo around the moon that will make you sick. Control yourself, control your passion.'

He asked me to shake the stone and the shell together again. So I repeated the operation about thirty times, but something seemed to interfere.

Taking some cowries from a small bag, he threw them on the table and examined their pattern. Occasionally he would sing under his breath, in Yoruba.

'Very interesting Legba.'

He tossed the cowries down again.

'What kind of a freak is that? Left hand.'

I opened my left hand. It was the shell again.

'No! Shake and separate again.'

We repeated the procedure several times.

When I at last produced the black stone, he said:

'Yes! Your Legba is an Elaki Legba. You will also have to wear a chain around your neck, with something attached to it. I am trying to learn what it is but he won't answer.'

He tossed the cowries down again. I shook the shell and the black stone together and separated them.

'I've got it! I know what it is. Unbelievable! I'll explain it to you. Legba is the keystone of the Yorubas. Legba is a bohemian who wears a Brooks Brothers suit. Legba is change! Legba is the tricks of life. For instance, a guy falls from a roof on another guy and kills him. OK, that's Legba!

'Let's say there are fifty million Yorubas in the world, in Africa, here, in Cuba, in Haiti, and in Brazil; each of them possesses a Legba. It's some kind of guardian angel. There aren't three who have the same as yours. It's a very rare Legba, very wild. It can be extremely useful to you.

'You must get this Legba and a chain, but you will have to feed it from time to time with chicken blood every month, or maybe more often if you find yourself in difficulty. We will have to initiate you to Legba, never mind the other Voodoos. Legba is not some kind of grigri or fetish; he is the way you look at the world and your walking stick.'

He described to me the fabrication of the Legba he was going to make and asked me to call him in two weeks.

'You must protect your body just as much as your mind.' And he added this sentence, which, today, sounds to me strangely meaningful:

'You want to be the King of the Kingdom but don't forget that you cannot enjoy the Kingdom in a wheelchair.'

It was at about the same time that I began to paint a large picture representing a black man seen from the waist up leading a horse, of which only the head and chest were visible.

Originally, the subject had been entirely different. The picture was supposed to represent a rich woman, in a fur coat, leading her horse; in short, an illustration of selfishness and money. To my great amazement, a black man with a naked, muscular torso appeared instead of this woman.

The picture was finished quite quickly, except for one detail. Impossible to paint the eyes of either the man or the animal; or, rather, more precisely, I painted them and the canvas immediately lost all meaning. The more I looked at it, the more aware I was of having created, in some way, a self-portrait.

That man and that somewhat crazy horse represented two aspects of my personality.

Finally, I left the canvas white where the horse's eyes belonged, and I rubbed the man's eyes lightly with a Kleenex, which had the effect of covering the sockets with skin, as if the eyelids were as joined together as mine are today.

When my wife, Idanna, from whom I was separated, moved my belongings after the accident, she came back to the hospital and mentioned the picture, which I had forgotten about. She described the shock she had when she went back into the studio and found herself face to face with those two blind creatures.

To paint such a subject before losing one's eyesight is, to say the least, a very strange coincidence.

And then, a week before the mugging, I woke up one morning in a state of anguish. A sentence echoed in my head: 'I am in danger.' I felt myself skidding. I was no longer like an animal in his own territory. I was already feeling so lost that I went to talk to the priests of my religion, not because I believe in their God but simply because I had been talking far too much to the priests of the other gods.

In this city of New York, smothered by material things, I had to meet someone who bases his life on spiritual practice, whatever his belief might be. I therefore went to see the Park Avenue Jesuits, the order that had educated me. But that day all they wanted was to show me the richness of their church and the names of donors engraved in gold on marble slabs.

I looked at that Jesuit with the eyes I still had while the sentence 'I am in danger' kept flashing back to me. But his red face, bloated and overfed, remained indifferent.

Yes, maybe I am unfair, but I am seized with a kind of anger when I think about it or when I think about God. And what I call God is probably not what you call God. But it is precisely against that God, yours, theirs, that my anger rises. My God is a God of indifference, without compassion or human feelings, which have nothing to do with the creation of the world, the creative principle, the life principle. My God is the God of Aho, that old Voodoo priest I lived with in Dahomey, who said to me:

'There's no point in praying to God; to pray is to belittle him. It is a ridiculous presumption. God will change nothing; he has decided everything in advance. You will be born, you will live, you will die. Nothing can be changed. I was born, I am living, and I will die. One must turn to the deities, the Voodoos, the ancestors. That's why there is the cult of the dead. The Creator will no longer come on earth.'

Perhaps that Jesuit priest saw in my eyes this cry for help. Embarrassed, he turned away.

'You know, you will not find here, among us, the same quality of men that you knew in Europe.' I felt puzzled by this remark.

Three hours later, after visiting the church from top to bottom, the three libraries, the new classrooms, the dining hall, and the kitchens, I found myself in the street again, more lost than ever.

I was in danger and what terrified me most was the absolute certainty that all the inner strength in me had disappeared. I felt a spiritual void and an inability to cope.

THREE

No one wants to or can accept my version:

'I went out for an evening walk around Washington Square before going to bed. I returned home. I was attacked by two unknown men.' Impossible! Impossible for the police.

Detective Marzoto came the day after the attack and again on following days. I could feel his suspicion. He made me repeat endlessly the order of the events, hoping that I would contradict myself, and wrote a report that had nothing to do with my statements. There were some errors in it, including certain serious ones, such as saying that I had opened the door to the attackers, implying that I knew them. 'That's what you told the police the night of the attack.' I knew that wasn't true. But why did he want to make me say that? What was he trying to prove? Vengeance, a homosexual crime? His mind was definitely working in that direction. I told him he was wasting his time. I was exhausted. A doctor came into the room and, before I realised what was happening, made an anal examination. Why? To find out if I was homosexual, to determine whether I had been raped? I was sure that it was at the request of the police.

I am on the VIP floor under special protection. The police fear something. Not I. There are journalists downstairs, eager for a story. I refuse to see them. Television and the *New York Times* have reported the attack, with incorrect details. I am described as somebody rich and important. I sense that people don't believe me.

A relative of mine who is in town for a few days calls me from the Hotel Pierre and this extraordinary conversation ensues:

'I would have liked to come see you, but I can't find a taxi.'

Here's a man who has built a business empire but who suddenly can't manage to come forty blocks downtown.

'What has happened to you is certainly dreadful, but you know, growing old is no fun either. To see less and less hair on your head every morning.'

'Yes, Enrico, I understand. Thanks for calling me.'

Months later, I learned that before phoning me he had called the police, who told him that some details of the case remained unclear. He went back to Europe with his version: drug dealing!

Some journalist friends of mine, outraged by these false rumours, offered to write an article exposing him. I refused, but I was sorely tempted.

Homosexual, raped, and a drug dealer! What was yet to come was the allegation that I was a sorcerer involved in black magic. For that matter, it wasn't the first time I had been accused of sorcery.

After a year in Africa, back in New York I missed the world of Aho. On the street I would look at black people. Did they remember where they came from? Dahomey? the Yoruba Empire? Our eyes never met, or met too quickly, out of fear.

Harlem, the forbidden city. I was sure that the Voodoos were alive there. Perhaps someone up there still continues the teaching of Aho. But how could I make contact? True, I had run into a Haitian guard at the Museum of Modern Art who recognised my initiatory rings.

Voodoo, black magic, blood, ritual murders. Those clichés clutter up everyone's subconscious. How am I to explain, that for me, Voodoo means peace, laughter, poetry, and inner harmony?

One morning, called by some force, I went up to the Schomburg Center in Harlem, determined to stay there as long as need be. Something was due to happen. In the reading room I was the only white person.

After two hours, a woman sat down at the same table, with a book. She wore African clothes. She looked at me and said:

'What are you studying?'

'Voodoo. Actually, I want to know if they exist in Harlem.'

She smiled.

'I myself am a daughter of Ogun.'

'You mean a wife of Ogun.'

'How do you know those things?'

I showed her a ritual object, given to me by Aho.

'You look like a Yoruba. Your clothes.'

'I am a Yoruba.'

'You were born?'

'In Harlem.'

She half opened the top of her garment and showed me bead necklaces in the colours of Ogun.

Her name was Alicia.

Strange weeks ensued. Little by little, Alicia introduced me to her religious family. Often she would speak to me of a certain Dwike, their spiritual father, the Godfather. She observed me.

One evening, I was rubbed from head to foot with a beef tongue. Then the tongue was rolled around a paper with writing on it and held in place with a wooden needle. Later we went out and threw it away at the nearest intersection, where Legba, who is also the Voodoo of crossroads, stands.

On another day, I picked Alicia up at her home, on 108th Street. We went to a market between Second and Third avenues where live chickens are sold. For twelve dollars we bought three white roosters. I carried two in a box and Alicia took the other one. She had brought along Olodoumé, her four-year-old son.

We went to where Dwike's mother lived, a few blocks away. The elevator was out of order and the staircase smelled of spicy cooking.

At the far end of the apartment was a small bedroom full of books and drums, some as big as barrels. Alicia threw herself to the floor and touched it with her forehead, then alternately with each shoulder.

In a corner of the room there was a shrine with several fetishes. On the black tile floor was my Legba, which I recognised from the way Dwike had described it during the divination. Three small wooden stakes were stuck in an earth-filled pot. It was an Elaki Legba or wooden Legba. Alongside, there was a small Legba which like mine also seemed quite fresh. It had

cowries representing eyes and mouth. Dwike had evidently fed
his Legba along with mine so as not to create any jealousy. At
the opening of the shrine stood a square stone covered with
dried blood. 'That is my business-Legba. The stone represents
a building because I'm in real estate.'

The first rooster was pulled from the box. Dwike plucked
some feathers from its neck and threw them on the Legbas.
Then he twisted its head off. Blood spurted out on the ritual
objects. The other two roosters were sacrificed in the same
way. He filled his mouth with rum and sprayed it on the shrine,
making a face:

'Shit! It burns. I'm not used to it. I don't drink alcohol.'

He lit a cigar and knelt down.

The floor was now covered with blood and feathers.

'Fuck, man, one thing is sure: this is a peasants' religion. In
an apartment it creates a hell of a mess.'

He put the lighted end of the cigar in his mouth and blew
smoke on the two Legbas. A candle, honey, and some fruits of
African origin were arranged as offerings.

'Observe carefully how I do this; every time you have to feed
your Legba, you must do the same.'

And then I was back in the subway, unsuccessfully trying to
conceal with newspaper this object dripping with blood.

A month later, Dwike came to MacDougal Alley to help me
'refresh' my Legba.

The ceremony took place in the narrow entry of the little
house because Legba is also the Voodoo of the threshold.

After blowing cigar smoke on the Legba, Dwike stood up and
said:

'All right! You'll clean up all this shit. I have an appointment,
I'm already late.'

He opened the door and froze. In front of him, my neighbour
was letting his dog have a pee. When he took in the spectacle
before him, roosters with their throats cut, the Legba streaming
with blood, the coconuts, the candle still burning, his mouth
opened for a shout that wouldn't come out.

Dwike turned around and burst out laughing.

'Oh, my God, did you see the look on his face?'

It was only later that my neighbour's mouth opened again to relate this incident to the police.

Voodoo, sorcery, black magic; some people insisted on looking there to find some explanation for the attack. However, the facts are completely different.

From the very first day in this hospital Aho has been present. He installs himself at the foot of my bed as he would on his own African mat. Our dialogue is incessant. Sometimes he rudely interrupts my conversations with visitors and friends. It is easy for him to do so because I'm the only one who sees and hears him, and he takes advantage of the situation: 'She doesn't know what she's saying. She has a dirty mind; don't listen.' The curve of his mouth, which is like a Benin bronze's, expresses scorn. He just sits there, wearing his curious cap, on which is appliquéd the lion of King Glé-Glé, the bull of Ghézo, and the shark of Béhanzin. He is wrapped up in his ceremonial buttercup yellow and pomegranate red cloak. Aho, my African father who taught me gut laughter, volcanic laughter, Aho the devourer of life, Aho the dancer, Aho the prince, Aho the Voodoo High Priest who initiated me. For months, on that former slave coast, I lived in his palace of misery. Endless nights I listened, under the immense star studded sky, to the teaching of dying old Africa. For months I followed him in the palm groves and the bushes to penetrate the secret of the convents. With him, I met the sorcerers, the 'charlatans,' the priestesses, the Voodoos, the positive and negative Forces. 'Every rock, every river, every plant, every person bears the visible mark of divine creation and of its dependence on the Creator. This signature of Mahù, the Architect, the Giver, is the shadow. I will teach you to see the invisible world.'

In this hospital room, Aho looks at me and his eyes are filled with love. He looks at me in that pose I know so well, with one finger placed against his temple, on which are etched three incisions, souvenirs of the male panther, the Agassu, who seized the king's daughter on the riverside and, in the throes of pleasure, left three scratches on each of the young girl's temples. Now they are the sign of recognition of all the Sons of Agassu, the Fon People. His face has that immovable look of bronze he wears on serious occasions.

'Aho, what would you do in my place?'

'It is very grave. You have been swimming in the waters of death and your life will never again be the same, but I know the Forces. Have confidence in me.'

He takes my thumb and sucks it as a sign of making a solemn oath, as has been the custom for centuries in the Kingdom of Abomey.

'That object which you forgot under the staircase in MacDougal Alley, your Legba, can only be neutralised by the sea. Someone must go and throw it there right away.'

I am sure of nothing. Nevertheless, I ask Michael to pick up the Legba. Going home that evening on the Staten Island Ferry, he will throw it overboard.

What disturbs me is that a week later, Michael came down with glaucoma.

It's as if my inner eyelids have been torn out. There is nothing that can interrupt this face to face confrontation within myself.

FOUR

It is more than a month that I have been in this hospital, and time has undergone a slight distortion.

I bathe my eyes with artificial tears, which I carry in a little bottle attached like an amulet to the string of my pyjama top. I finally arranged to keep the bottle with me because the nurses continually forgot this simple treatment. And yet it is an essential procedure, which can prevent the dehydration of my burned eyes and their complete devitalisation, which would annul any future chance of recovery. My eyes should have been moistened at least an hour ago. I ring. 'Later.' Later no one comes. I ring again. 'Oh, I'm sorry. I forgot.' The nurse leaves and doesn't come back. There has been a change of shift. A new nurse arrives. I begin my request all over again. Fury consumes me, as does weariness from having to fight to obtain these treatments. I think that this neglect is due to indifference, which is probably incorrect, but the consequences can be so serious that my anger is justified. The nurses, who have grown rather accustomed to my good humour, are astonished.

I feel curiously high, a kind of drowsiness overcomes me in midmorning. I feel dumb; my brain doesn't work. Psychic reaction? Perhaps, but I have my doubts, and one morning when they bring me, as they do every day, some pills in a paper cup, 'pills to improve your digestion, to stimulate your stomach,' my fingers grope: two long capsules and two small, round tablets with a groove in the middle. The size, the indentation make me suspicious.

'And what is that?'

'Valium.'

'I never asked for Valium.'

'The doctor prescribed it.'

I take the two pills and drop them in the ashtray.

'From now on there's no point in giving me the Valium. I'll throw it away.'

'You're making a mistake. It would help you stay calm and able to handle the psychological shock.'

'If I need any, I'll ask for some.'

What right does the doctor have to smuggle a drug like Valium into my body without letting me know? The result is that I have been in a state of anguish over the drowsiness in my brain. And the way my head and my mind were deserting me seemed like a cowardly act of my subconscious. I accepted, as something temporarily necessary, that weakness of a part of myself that I did not control.

I naturally feel much better since stopping the Valium and that is no doubt what makes it possible for me to write today.

This morning, as usual, they wheel me to the treatment room. The aide, who is new, hands me a magazine, saying:

'Be patient. There are a lot of people.'

I take the magazine to avoid embarrassing him, and the smell of printer's ink gives me a tremendous appetite for reading.

Two fingers on my shoulder and the voice of Dr T:

'I have to talk to you.'

I am surprised at the warm intensity he communicates to me by the pressure of his fingers, even though his voice remains cold. This finger language has been established between us over the course of the past days.

Idanna shows up and asks to come along with me. He agrees, with what seems to me like relief, and pushes my wheelchair to his office.

I already know that something is wrong. The animal in me can smell it. His monotonous voice informs me:

'Your eyes are not doing well. The tissues are dissolving and I fear perforation. I must perform an ablation of the left eye.'

I sustain a colossal punch in the stomach. I feel nauseous. Without understanding its complete meaning, I know that this sentence announces something horrible. I hear the same horror in Idanna's voice:

'Would it be possible to give one of my eyes so that he will be able to see?'

'It would be useless; one person's eye cannot be grafted onto someone else.'

'But perhaps later?'

'No, it will never be possible.'

He even seems shocked at such a proposal.

Thank God, this kind of choice is spared us. How difficult it would be to accept such a mutilation! I feel Idanna would be capable of it and that disturbs me.

I try not to confuse courage and pride. Not to stand like a cathedral whose closed doors conceal its collapsed vault. I am also wary of that indulgence people feel obliged to lavish on someone in my condition.

I continue to moisten my eyes myself, but since Dr T.'s news, I feel like a gardener watering dead flowers.

For the last two days, since knowing that my left eye is to be removed, I have this fear in my stomach, a disgust for my body, which will be irrevocably mutilated. I have this continually recurring image of a small spoon detaching an oyster from its shell and of a mouth gulping it down. This mutilation seems to me a further plunge into darkness, a thickening of the nightmare, a process of degradation that cannot be halted. Luck, that famous luck of mine which has always saved me at the brink of catastrophe, has definitely forsaken me this time.

I feel like a Kamikaze pilot who has been shot down. Perhaps my vaguely Japanese pyjamas and the black blindfold I wear to hide my cooked-fish eyes have something to do with it. Behind this black bandeau, I hide the wound that seems to me too intimate to be exposed to just anybody's gaze. Modesty and a feeling of vulnerability force me to take shelter, to hide behind this blindfold which also makes me look like someone about to be executed. Being masked makes me feel as if I am reestablishing some degree of equality with the person I'm talking to. I

can't look him in the eyes, but neither can he scrutinise me
without my being aware of it.

An obsessive image keeps coming back: a man's head, a
plaster or perhaps alabaster head. The head stands out against
an intensely blue sky, blue like the sky when you fly above the
clouds. The man's head is white and has a kind of transparency.
His eyes are wide open, also white, and on these two white
globes there is the very black design of a labyrinth. These black
lines are the small cracks I see at the back of my eye, on the
retina, when I look at the sun or when the doctors examine me
with their little penlight. But it is also the design of the labyrinth
of darkness in which I now feel imprisoned. This labyrinth with
its twists and turns, dead ends, and walls which I bump against
as soon as I want to believe I'm free. As soon as I let myself be
invaded by claustrophobia and the despair that blackness brings,
I hear resounding in the passageways, as in the convolutions of
my brain, the growling of a monstrous beast, a blind Minotaur.

I also dream of a sightless knight whose visor is stuck. The
knight rides along, with his sword held out before him. He is
filled with distrust and fear because he can no longer see. A
young girl advances towards him, her gentle face surrounded
by fair, luminous hair. Between her slender fingers she seizes
the sword. The man trembles but the fierce steel conveys to
his heart the message of love. He leans from his horse and,
grasping her by the waist, he places her in front of him. In this
way they ride for days and days. Faint with love, she leans
against the metal that encloses him. He is deep in silence. They
reach a vast forest, the domain of the sightless knight. The
animals come out to greet them. Silently, the knight draws from
his chain mail a long, delicately sharpened dagger and slowly
pierces the heart of the young girl, who, through love, submits
herself totally to this supreme act. She slips from the saddle,
life leaving her, and collapses alongside the road. She sees the
knight move off, surrounded by a halo of light, while darkness
descends within her.

At times, I am afraid that the memory I have of the visible world
is disappearing little by little, to be replaced by an abstract

universe of sound, smell, and touch. I force myself to visualise the bedroom with its metal furniture, its window, the curtains. I bring to mind paintings, Rembrandt's Polish cavalier, Francis Bacon's portraits of Innocent X.

My ability to create images absolutely must not atrophy. I must remain capable of bringing back the world I looked at intensely for thirty-five years. By contemplating in my memory the volcano of Lombok or the perfect harmony of a building designed by Michelangelo, I continue to receive instruction and knowledge from them. That is the immense privilege of blind people who were formerly able to see.

This morning, under the cold shower that relaxes me from the night's tensions, I suddenly say to myself:

'What the hell! What difference does it make? As long as they save the right one. As long as I still have the hope of seeing with at least one eye. What's the importance of the left eye being dead, here in its socket or in a garbage can! In any case, I have no choice.'

I don't want to bother with my eyes any longer. I don't want anyone to talk to me about them. I let others be responsible for treating them with balm. I don't want to go on being the gardener of these dead flowers. The others see only the closed petals, but I know very well that the pistil is dead.

I am between death and birth. I am dead to my past life and not yet reborn to this new one. This whole period is merely an extraordinary labour through which I am giving birth to myself.

FIVE

It is early July and a heat wave pushes the thermometer up to over 100 degrees Fahrenheit. Saint Vincent's Hospital, in Greenwich Village, is one of New York's oldest. Such a temperature makes the absence of air conditioning unbearable. In the space of a few days, the ward seems much quieter. 'A lot of our clients have left for the weekend' is the hypocritical explanation. Off on a camping trip under their oxygen tents! I suppose.

Here black humour is probably a necessary antidote. Inadvertently, I left my tape recorder going on my bedside table while I was taking a shower and thus recorded the conversation of two female aides while they were making my bed. Besides some good points they granted me, they found my sense of humour completely deplorable. 'It's a pity he likes such bad jokes!'

The heat level rises and I ask for a drawer in the morgue while Mr Schwartz breathes the oxygen of higher altitudes under a plastic dome.

Mr Schwartz remains alive thanks to two holes, one for breathing, one for eating. When the nurse cleans them, there is a terrible gurgling noise, like water running out of a sink. This is the only manifestation of Mr Schwartz's existence that I would ever be able to perceive.

The television set goes nonstop from 8:00 A.M. until three o'clock the following morning. Mr Schwartz's eyes are closed, I am told; he's asleep. Let's turn off the television. A rumbling sound informs me immediately that Mr Schwartz, awakened by the absence of television, is in a state of panic. Mr Schwartz is filled with panic; quick, turn the television back on. The gurgling sound stops. The oxygen whistles. Detective Kojak's voice continues the eternal, identical scenario: 'Take him in or shoot him but I don't want to hear any more about it.'

Mr Schwartz has closed his eyes, appeased. An adjustable bracket presents the set to him at the correct angle, the ideal height, in perfect position. When are you going to die, Mr Schwartz? I share totally the impatience of your family, who come less and less frequently and don't even bother to lower the volume of the television. I can't smoke, because it will blow up the oxygen tent. So when are they going to disconnect that tent and fold up that bracket? When are you going to kick the bucket, Mr Schwartz? That's the question we ask ourselves, the nurses and your family and myself.

Mr Schwartz gave us satisfaction in the middle of a soap opera. I heard a gurgling sound that wasn't very clean. Mr Schwartz was vomiting his liver before leaving.

The most atheistic death I could have imagined.

A Jesuit father has replaced Mr Schwartz and his is a completely different case. He shivers and asks for blankets. First his foot was amputated, then his knee. The gangrene seems to have been checked. They make him sit in an armchair. He never protests, is perfectly submissive. Only this time, in a plaintive voice, he asks for his chair to be placed so that he can see me better. I am surprised and flattered by this sudden attention, but not for long. As soon as the nurse disappears, I hear him clutching at the metal bedrail, perhaps at the trapeze bar left there since his operation.

You make me laugh, Father; you're like one of your dunces in Manila. To see Hugues better? that's what you said, Father.

Here we are, I hear the bed creak as you sigh with pleasure at having your eyes once again turned towards the sky. The smell of shit fills the room. Father can no longer control his sphincter. With his eyes lost in the clouds of his prayers, Father is unaware of the shit running down his legs and the sickening smell. The smell of your shit doesn't bother me, Father. To the female aide who pushed you around because you should have rung the bell and not shit in bed, I say, 'Give him a break.'

She gets back at him by handling his stump roughly, prevented by her stupidity and weariness from seeing the beauty of Father, the beauty of this man.

'Oh! . . . Hmm! . . .'

The moans remain stuck in Father's throat.

Summer is settling in. People, friends leave on vacation. There are fewer visits. The heat becomes ingrained.

The Jesuit is completely silent except for a few sighs in his sleep. Never a complaint. He doesn't even hear the telephone ring on his bedside table. I reach over the railing of my bed, which is raised on his side, and locate the phone by the sound.

'Hello . . . Father, telephone.'

He comes out of his drowsiness, his dreams, his prayers, his heaven:

'Yes, yes, oh! thank you.'

A woman comes every day to shave him and to recite the rosary with him. I hear the sound of water in the basin and the woman's monologue: 'There, Father, you're going to be a handsome boy, turn your head, Father. No, the other way. This blade doesn't cut anymore, Father. Why do you have your eyes closed?' And he says nothing but 'Hmm, hmm.'

'Hail Mary, full of grace . . . Why do you have that look on your face, Father? You're going to frighten the nurses . . . full of grace, the Lord is with thee . . . I made an apple pie last night. I brought some for you, but I don't know if you deserve it, you bad boy . . . Blessed art thou amongst women . . . you are asleep, Father! Oh, good Lord what a look you have. That's better, you're smiling . . . and blessed is the fruit of thy womb, Jesus . . .'

She would leave around four o'clock.

Writing tires me but relieves me as well. The days are long, monotonous. I invent a kind of discipline for myself.

I have excellent classical music, German, Indian, Chinese, Japanese, African. But I can't listen to it in peace and quiet because there is a constant coming and going of all sorts of people in this room: lawyers, the police, the French consul; Anna, who, in spite of her thoroughly British modesty, opens her blouse to let me caress her breasts, which she had brought me instead of flowers.

And Richard Neville, constantly obscene since winning his famous lawsuit.

'How do you say, in French, to suck a cock?'

'Faire une pipe.'

'Yes, yes, that's it!'

Sorry, Father; take this glass of Mouton-Rothschild to allow me to be pardoned for having such friends. And you would drink that glass without comment, without passing judgment, with love.

For there has been love between this Jesuit Father and me.

I brought him my zest for life in spite of everything, though he had only one idea: to die. I felt this in his total indifference to his condition or to his colleagues' Irish jokes.

'So, Father, now that the doctor has said that in a few days you'll be able to rejoin the parish's soccer team.'

This kind of humour seems to arouse only scorn in Father. No, Father wants to die. In the evening I suspect that he prays to his God to call him. If I bring him my frenzied desire to live, he brings me his serenity. I see him as a figure of light. You don't give a damn about how your stump is coming along. Worse still, you let yourself be dragged along every day for rehabilitation without participating in it. For the circulation in your legs, you mustn't lie stretched out for hours in your bed.

One morning, I have a papaya put on his breakfast tray, to remind him of the Philippine Islands, where for more than fifteen years he taught Latin.

'Oh, Dios, una papaya!'

I hear him murmur *una papaya*.

Without a word we have, curiously, communicated.

In the course of a month, he would speak to me three times.

The first time, he asked me:

'About your eyes, is it temporary or permanent?'

'It's temporarily permanent.'

'I will pray for you.'

Thank you, Father.

The second conversation took place about ten days later. I was asleep and, all of a sudden, was awakened by the strangely firm voice of the Jesuit Father calling out:

'Nurse, nurse!'

'So, Father, what do you want?'

'I want my breakfast; it's already past ten and no one has come.'

'It's ten P.M., Father, not time for breakfast.'

'Are you sure?'

'Look out the window, Father!'

'Ah yes! Ah yes, you're right.'

And he went back to sleep, rather embarrassed.

The third conversation occurred when he was leaving for a rest home, a place for dying, and I knew I was losing a companion of such a special quality.

As they were wheeling him to the door, he said to me:

'Well, Hugues, so long. It was a real pleasure to share my room with you.'

'I'm sorry I can't say the same. But you have been so odious that my only consolation is the thought of what the Japanese did to you.'

He must have been surprised that I knew about that episode in his life. He had been interned and tortured by the Japanese for three years.

I could hear his laughter as they wheeled him down the corridor.

SIX

The nights are long, monotonous.

Makassar arose out of my nights of insomnia, fear, and suffering. Makassar, which has no more reality than a dream, a utopia. When I'm finished with the hospital, I will go to Makassar. I know nothing of this city except for the tales of the Bugis sailors, and a white coast on the horizon.

For a week we fought against the winds on that turtle-fishing boat. I saw wild islands, women with gold teeth and sexes like sea anemones. I saw a white-hot island where lepers eat sharks. I saw dark islands hiding in the night, imprisoned in their own magic. Only the wind swept me along, for I had no wish to see nature in the raw, crude savagery, man without hope, whitened bones in the lagoons, children wasting away, the thousand rupee young girl, the rotting shark gazing at the leper, and all the wrecks of our gutted dreams in the cove of no return.

At the end of every day Pa-Suni, the captain, would thrust his fist towards the hazy line of land and say 'Makassar!' before ordering the manoeuvre that would take us away on a new tack. His voice, when he pronounced the name Makassar, took on an intonation that contained the whole city, the bars, the brothels, the stabbings, the prahus arriving from every corner of that liquid country, that floating nation, those fourteen thousand islands spread between the archipelago of Java, Borneo, the Celebes, and the Philippines.

But Makassar was a myth in the captain's head, as it is in mine tonight. Never will I reach Makassar, never will I attain Makassar. No more than we reached it with our boat. Winds, currents, a typhoon join forces to keep me at a distance from the mirage. I must learn patience. After days of useless struggle with the wind to reach Makassar, old Abdul Jemal said: 'When your life depends on the wind, a great calmness descends within you.'

Why do I need this mirage if it isn't to calm my fear, my claustrophobia, when I think of the narrow life of a disabled cripple? The lie doesn't deceive me. This metal bed drowns immediately in this voyage of hope. The sails of my dreams are torn and I remain beached on my sheets. Physical suffering is bearable. But my fevers take source elsewhere. I am finished, finished.

I grope for the bell. Nine minutes go by, then a dragging footstep.

'Yes!'

'I'm in pain, give me a shot of Demerol.'

'We can't give you that regularly; you'd become addicted to it.'

Or sometimes they give it to me without any discussion. Then everything relaxes, I feel good, I am warm, my limbs stretch out, the tension leaves my neck. I will have all the courage I need. I smile, I wish someone were here so we could enjoy a good talk about Stendhal's travel diaries, for instance, or David Maloof's poems.

Makassar, the challenge no longer seems necessary. I accept without suffering the verdict imposed by the contrary wind and the cyclone that dismasted me. The drug flows smoothly in my veins, with tenderness, and I abandon myself without remorse, without fear. I don't have the makings of a junkie, I'm not afraid of letting myself get hooked. Take a rest from this nightmare from which you cannot escape. Mozart, in my headphones, takes charge of my body and carries it into a world of sensations without landscape.

If they refuse to give me a shot, I say nothing, out of pride and because I'm curious to see just how deep I'm going to sink. I listen to the noises of the abyss, I expect at any time the intrusion of cold, blind monsters. I sink. The pressure rises. My lungs no longer swell. The darkness is total, liquid, palpable. It enters through my nose, my ears, my mouth; it envelops my

body, penetrates it. I breathe it in jerky gasps. I know I am
going to crack. But when? Tonight? I listen to the approach of
the monsters. The sooner the better. But an animal force
maintains and will maintain what I pompously call the state of
grace.

I eat like a soldier, not for nourishment but for endurance. In
two months I have put on more than twenty pounds. My body
is already changing. A blind man's body, heavy, slow, not very
flexible. The metamorphosis horrifies me. Only my hands have
grown thinner, more supple. 'Your hands have changed,' a
doctor tells me.

I don't break many things, rarely knock them over. I am
learning how to use the back of my fingers, how to analyse in
an instant the message received, how to be so discreet in my
gropings that they become imperceptible. The same training as
in horseback riding, where the hand and leg seem motionless.
Vanity? No! Refusal to become debased, simple respect for
man. Dignity is a common share, a part of which is entrusted to
me.

Night is going to collapse. What is the point of this battle for
hope? I am doomed. The evidence echoes in my head. I will
never be able to reach Makassar. You are lying to yourself. You
are escaping into unreality. Makassar is a mythical city. For
you, there is no more Makassar.

The next morning, I say to my friend Patrick, who knows
those regions and what is to be found there:

'As soon as I'm finished with the hospital, I'll go to Makassar!'

'Yes, why not? Good idea!'

I am astonished at his not being astonished. There's some
trap there. Perhaps he is saying that to me the way you humour
a madman:

'Sure, sure, you are Napoleon!'

What is obvious is that the adventure that creates freedom and
provides answers can no longer be pursued in the same way.
And in any case, in order to go further, I definitely had to change.
Adventure is revolt, not to be resigned, the opposite of cynicism.

By adventure I mean everything that is opposed to the loss of consideration for life. No injury is irreparable except for the despair of Judas. To be free is to avoid being moulded by an epoch, a race, a civilisation, a religion, a social caste, or one's own psyche. A renouncement of whatever is individual for the essential. Every character in the Bible has an individual reality, a history, but it is their ensemble, the Bible, which is revealing. What happened to me has happened to all of humanity and what is undergone in Cambodia and the prisons of Argentina is undergone by me as an individual. But that will come about only when I have assumed totally, very humbly, my complete dimension as a man. To attain one's dimension as a man is the very goal of the adventure, the end of the road.

Old Abdul Jemal, on the Bugis boat, told me:

'Of little importance is the port, for it will always be necessary to sail off again. Only the crossing counts.'

SEVEN

I feel much blinder than I did a few days ago. I perceive less
and less light. My obscurity is more opaque. My eyes hurt.
Vulnerable to stabbing pains, apoplexy, they are like two plastic
bags full of water and ready to fall to the floor when I lean over.
The burn is so deep, Dr T. has told me, that he is afraid there'll
be a perforation at any moment.

Even before the doctor gave me the sickening news, I had
noticed a change in the nurses. A serious nuance in their voices,
a grave nuance hiding behind trivial conversation. The nurses
from other wards also would come to see me, and that sudden
attention alerted the animal in me. It smelt of danger. Now that
they know I am aware of the situation and they see that my
behaviour hasn't changed, they relax and I no longer hear in
their voices the graveness of the secret.

We are waiting for the Fourth of July weekend to pass. It is,
on the roads, one of the most murderous weekends in the year
and the Eye Bank will have a superabundance of stock. Dr T.
is waiting to be able to choose the most appropriate tissues to
perform the grafts he hopes will prevent the right eye from
bursting.

Aho is dead and I didn't know about it. I found out by a
telephone call from an African friend. He died a few weeks ago;
we don't know the exact date. And yet Aho is here during these
days of waiting, sitting at the foot of my bed. I ask him:

'Are you dead?'

He waves his hand, as if chasing away a fly.

'It's of no importance. The world of the dead is like the world
of the living.'

'They're going to operate on me and remove my left eye.'

'You need strength and courage.' Aho gazes scornfully at the hospital food. 'Looks like an albino chicken. What you should have is some heart and penis of a lion like the ones sold by the Nagos hunters in the market of Abomey, but in this city of slaves they know nothing. The penis is the road to God.'

I listen to this man who, according to what they said in Africa, had cast a spell on me. It's true. Aho has cast a love spell on me. His voice calms me, reassures me, and opens up the invisible world to me. I reach for a cigarette and knock over the ashtray for the third time today. My morale is affected. I feel like hurling the water jug against the wall or crying, but his laughter, which comes from his guts rather than his throat, soothes me and wins me over.

The intern has come to get me, as he does every morning, and pushes me in a wheelchair to the treatment room. A little girl who also comes every day to have an infected cornea treated shouts at the doctor:

'Why do you put pepper in my eye?'

This time it isn't Dr T. who examines me. I hear the masculine voice of a woman as she walks towards me. Then a hand lifts up my head by pushing me under the chin, a light shines first in my left and then in my right eye.

'Will you clean up this garbage!' says the woman doctor with disgust. The intern, without saying a word, guides me towards the table on which stands that hard apparatus I now know so well. I put my head in it slowly, with precaution, and place my chin on the chin rest, as the light flares up again. Using a delicate steel instrument, the intern cuts the filaments of flesh that grow like buds every night, connecting the eye to the eyelid. A job requiring patience on his part as well as mine. He pours a liquid in my eye, wipes it with what seems like a cotton pad, then goes on cutting. At first, I had a hard time taking these daily sessions, and then I developed a way of breathing that puts my brain to sleep. I absent myself, so to speak.

When the cleanup is at last finished, the intern takes me back to the woman doctor; the little penlight shines again.

'Do you see the light?'

'Yes.'

She moves the light.

'And now?'

'Yes, and now, yes.' It seems to me that this is the hundredth time I have been examined. The same questions, the same answers. Or maybe it's the same session, which has never stopped, which goes on indefinitely. I'm not even interested in it anymore. I answer mechanically. She covers my left eye. 'And now?' 'Yes.' She covers my right eye. 'And now?' 'Yes.' She speaks to the intern and explains in a peremptory tone that I am wrong, that actually I don't see anything with the left eye but that I imagine seeing the light. I interrupt her:

'No! I see the light with my left eye, really.'

'You believe you see the light, but that's not so. Actually, it's a normal reaction.'

My anger is flaring up. Every day in my room I submit both my eyes to tests that will tell me whether or not their sensitivity to light is weakening. I know that I see light with my left eye.

She goes on talking to me and, while pushing me under the chin to make me raise my head, she inadvertently sticks her finger in my eye. I put my head in my hands and shout out in pain.

'Hold on!' says this woman.

The quarter of Irish blood in my veins boils.

'Hold on?'

I jump to my feet from the wheelchair.

'When you stick your fingers in somebody's eye, you don't say, "Hold on"! I don't even know who you are; you have not even introduced yourself, you examine me like some animal at a fair. You call my eyes garbage and when you finally poke your finger in them, you don't apologise. Leave me alone. Take me back to my room!'

I sit back down in the wheelchair. There is a moment of silence, then I hear some steps moving away, the slam of a door, and suppressed laughter. The intern who wheels me quickly to my room tells me confidentially that the woman doctor is the head of interns in the Department of Ophthalmology. I can tell from his voice that he is delighted, but I can't get over my anger. 'The bitch, the fucking bitch,' I keep repeating to myself to let off steam.

Idanna is waiting in my room. I tell her everything that happened. We end up laughing at the whole scene.

'In any case, if you think they're wrong and that you really see light with your left eye, why don't you ask them to get a second opinion? I have the name of a very reputable doctor here in New York.'

When Dr T. comes by later in the afternoon, I ask him if he has any objection to my being examined by one of his colleagues. He hesitates, then he asks noncommittally:

'Are you thinking of any particular doctor?'

'Yes, Dr Muller.'

'No, I have no objection. I know Dr Muller well; we often work together and he's a friend. I'll get in touch with him myself if you'd like.'

Dr Muller is a young man, sporty, very energetic. Communication is easy with him. He came the following morning. There is no time to lose. Once again, the little light. 'And now?' 'Yes.' 'And now?' 'No . . . Yes . . . Yes . . . No' etc. First one eye is covered, then the other. Finally I hear the click that means he is turning off the penlight for good.

'You are absolutely right. You see light with both your eyes. It's a good sign as far as the optic nerve is concerned, and then, even if it's not much, it is important to try to preserve it for the future. Your left eye is indeed in very bad shape and runs the risk of being perforated at any moment and emptying itself. In that case, the only thing to do will be to remove it. I will recommend in my report that every possible effort be made to try to keep the left eye, since it sees light perfectly well.'

Sun! Sun! The nightmare of the empty socket, of mutilation, of the gulped-down oyster, of a part of myself thrown into a trash can on Greenwich Avenue and taken at dawn to the garbage dumps of New York, fades away. So what! What difference does this really make? No difference and a big difference. It isn't logical; it's animal. Even if they are dead, I want to keep my eyes. I want to die complete.

*   *   *

Later, I reply to Dr T., who has read his colleague's report and indicates to me that the chances of saving my left eye remain minimal:

'Listen, I don't give a damn even if I have to go back under the knife three days later because it hasn't worked and the eye gets perforated; we've got to try.'

He laughs; I don't know why.

Now everything is different. To hell with resignation! Defeat is not obligatory. The fight goes on. There is this suspense now. The operation is no longer merely a nasty sanitary measure. Hope hangs in suspense. Oh, no big deal, but a possible halt in this degradation, this putrefaction that has continued slowly, irrevocably, since the acid spurted into my eyes.

My hand squeezes Idanna's. Idanna, my faithful ally, who refuses to give up and who fights for me inch by inch, who has spent hours talking to lawyers, doctors, organisations that might help. The bills must be paid, and they are now becoming exorbitant. She has discovered a state agency called the Crime Victims Compensation Board, which covers the medical expenses of victims of crimes committed in New York State. Innocence must be proved. She spends afternoons in police offices compiling a file, examining Detective Marzoto's reports and contesting them. She now knows the facts as well as I do, but I sense that even she is not convinced. 'Later . . . later,' I tell myself when I get irritated by this incredulity.

My burned eyelids have a tendency to retract and turn inward. My eyeball is scratched by the lashes, or, more accurately, what is left of them, and that friction becomes a Chinese torture. I lose patience, bathe the eye, hold the eyelids away with my fingers.

It's getting later in the day; it is hot. This obsessive, constant irritation gradually invades me completely. I try to calm down, without success. Finally, I ask for some pain killers, but I have waited too long and they produce no effect. I ask for the doctor. It is Saturday; the intern on duty has already gone home. I try to reach Dr T. at the various numbers he has given me in case of emergency. An answering service replies that the doctor has gone away for the weekend to attend a convention in Dallas.

Night is one of those endless tunnels. I wait for morning, I wait for the intern's arrival. I count the seconds. The night nurse has refused to give me the shot of Demerol I asked for because it isn't indicated on my chart. Finally, morning comes, and so does the intern.

'I see only one solution,' says the young doctor, 'and that is cutting off the eyelashes.'

The pain is confined to the right eye because the edge of the upper and lower eyelids of the left one were completely eaten away by the acid and the lashes have disappeared.

'Cut them off, do anything as long as it stops the pain.'

He cuts. I am given drops to calm the irritation. My nerves relax. My back, my neck become less tense.

At noon, I am a ball of fire. That intern is an imbecile. Now, instead of being irritated by long, soft lashes, the eyeball is being scratched by a series of cut-off lashes, as hard as darts. My brain, after a few hours, is boiling with pain. I stick on a piece of adhesive tape that keeps the eyelids apart.

I spend the four days before my operation applying pieces of tape, which, because of the heat, slip and stretch. But again I notice that we can get used to anything; this pain gradually becomes normal, an integral part of everyday reality. It doesn't disappear, but my brain organises itself in such a way as to absorb it, channel it, digest it.

EIGHT

Two days have passed since Independence Day.

A nurse came this morning to take a blood sample. I had been expecting that as a sign that the operation would take place. It will happen this evening or tomorrow. I am ready, a little edgy. We are waiting for fresh tissues from the Eye Bank. Somewhere a corpse is being cut up for me. The nurses and I are waiting. I go about my preparation like a bullfighter, with my hair washed, my face shaved and freshened up with cologne. I arrange my clothes so they won't look too much like what they are: hospital pyjamas with a slit up the back to make going to the bathroom easier. I have always hated to pay hospital visits, mainly because of the way most patients let themselves go. The men especially. I am not sick but the victim of an accident; the rest of my body is in fine shape.

Every morning, as I take a cold shower, I hope to wash away the weariness that besieges me even before the day begins. Every morning, as I leave my dreams, which are the only moments during which my sight is restored, I face the disappointment of reality. Endlessly, every night, I dream that I have made a mistake, that the others are mistaken, that I almost went blind, that I thought I was blind. I see! I can see! My joy is immense. I see fields of wild flowers swept by the wind. How beautiful the Earth is! Waves of pleasure fill my body. My heart swells with relief. But no, I am not blind! I see the house where I was born, I go over every detail. The only disturbing thing is that the others don't seem to notice that I can see. They don't seem to have been told that it's a mistake, that I am not really blind. They do things in front of me that they wouldn't do if they knew that I could see them. They exchange looks about me, put on expressions of pity. I am embarrassed, as if I were guilty of committing an indiscretion by observing them.

When I wake up, I am at first incredulous. Yes, I know something happened, I don't see well. I have some difficulties, but not that bad! Not total darkness, not this complete absence of images.

Regularly, Idanna comes and helps me exercise by walking up and down the corridors. It has slowed down my organism to a tremendous extent. I feel my body being transformed, not to say deformed. I have tried to move around on my own, but progress is made difficult by patients walking around with their intravenous drips suspended from stands on wheels. After I crashed into a few, mixed up their tubes, and finally upset their life-giving elixir, the nurses took me in hand and refused to let me walk around alone outside my room. I went out right away, with the Jesuit Father's stand, to which I had attached a bottle of genuine French Bordeaux: After all, why not.

Idanna has discovered a terrace a few floors down. It's fairly cool there. One afternoon we come across a young doctor holding the hand of a boy sitting in a wheelchair. He is looking at him lovingly. Idanna, who knows how curious I am, describes the scene to me with her Florentine wit. The doctor, who must have noticed our interest, gets up and walks towards us. 'Would you like a joint?' he asks, holding out the thin cigarette he was smoking. New York! New York! Decadence or free spirit? Anyway, an incredibly alive city. On this terrace hit by the July sun, which inundates my tired brain with gold as soon as I remove my blindfold, gusts of wind bring the smell of the ocean. At the end of the terrace, a door leads into the chapel. Like all chapels in the world, it smells of wax and incense. We sit down on a wooden bench. The chapel is empty, and so am I. All I feel is a void. I ask for a bit of courage. The religious temptation awakens no echo in my soul; this silence suits me for the time being. I wonder whether Idanna is praying and I don't dare get up to leave.

From Europe, I have received two botttes of miraculous

water, one from San Damiano and the other from Lourdes. The
latter is particularly interesting. It is a plastic bottle representing
the Virgin. The head twists off to let the water flow out. One
of the cleaning women, a Jamaican, couldn't resist the temptation
and stole it from me. I felt relieved when I discovered its
disappearance, for deep within me there is this temptation: What
if it worked? You have nothing to lose. But on the contrary, I
feel I have something important to lose. I had the same feeling
when the Voodoo priests offered me protective charms, grigris.
Aho used to say, 'My grigris are in my guts.' Yes, it is within
ourselves that we must build our forces, our protections. If the
irrational overcomes me, I may lose myself in it. The decision
to pour one or the other, or a cocktail of both, never seemed
possible. Lack of humility? No, something that has to do with
respect for the human condition. I cannot allow myself to toy
with hope. The preservation of harmony between action and
knowledge. In Africa, I observed white people who, for their
amusement, indulged in magic. They always ended by losing
something and eventually became the prey of very sophisticated
manipulators. They were becoming weaker just as they thought
they were acquiring powers. Magic is certainly not the highest
form of dialogue with the spiritual world. I feel for it both a kind
of instinctive repulsion and at the same time a passionate quest.
From those months of searching under Aho's guidance, I
acquired the conviction that his magic world was not what is
ordinarily believed to be the magic world. He was extremely
distrustful of the latter, for he knew its boomerang effect perfectly well. He resorted to it only when immediate results were
required.

Since that blood sample, waiting is more acute. The sooner the
better, I repeat to myself.

There is also a doctor who comes to see me regularly. He's
a cancer specialist; he refuses to sit down and says nothing. I
feel myself being observed, which makes me uncomfortable.
Today he breaks the silence to say:

'I would hate for my life to be a tragedy, because, after all, I
have only one.'

'So do I,' echoes Idanna.

I keep silent, for they are right. I feel depressed. It is my life and even if I'm blind, I love it and refuse to recognise anyone's right to belittle it.

I distrust intellectuals just now. They ask questions, analyse, want me to analyse, and, ultimately, they judge.

A journalist friend of mine tells me:

'You gambled your life and you lost.'

I turn the sentence around in my head and find no meaning to it, no reality.

Aho, who is listening, grumbles:

'Let the wise guys and the chatterboxes ramble on. They claim to know everything, especially the unknowable.'

A representative of the French government comes to see me, strictly out of a sense of duty, and carries on a *mondaine* conversation.

'But, you know, people are doing things these days without having any idea of the consequences. Your case is, of course, a tragic example of that, but look at what they did in Versailles,' referring to the bomb that had exploded a few days earlier in the palace of the Sun King.

What an honour, having my eyes compared to the Sun King's ceilings. Oh, Alfred Jarry!

Yesterday evening, the intern came to see me. I was drowsing. He touched my arm. I jumped violently and then discovered that I was afraid. He had come to notify me that I would be operated on the next morning at ten o'clock. He had me sign a paper releasing the surgeon from responsibility in case of an accident.

As soon as I wake, the waiting begins. Ten-thirty. They are late. Eleven. The sound of a trolley being wheeled in the corridor warns me, and then the room is invaded. Sounds of metal. I raise myself onto the narrow, hard stretcher. They wrap my body up in thick linen. In the corridor the nurses wish me good luck. One of them is crying, which doesn't leave me much hope for my left eye. I wonder whether something has been hidden from me.

Idanna walks behind my head and strokes my forehead. We are late; the nurses wheel me along quickly. Doors close behind us. The anaesthetist shakes my hand, introduces himself, sticks a needle in my left arm. He jokes, speaks French:

'I did some of my studies in Paris. Ah, Paris! It's not like it is here!'

I hear a noise that clearly seems to me to be a slap on a buttock. And from the nurse, in French:

'Obsédé!'

'Hello, Monsieur de Montalembert!'

Dr T. has just come in. He fixes an apparatus to my head. I feel myself losing consciousness.

'Doctor, I think you can begin,' I say before dropping off, but I don't drop off and the surgeon's voice answers me, in the same polite way:

'It's over, Monsieur de Montalembert.'

I don't understand. I don't understand that between the moment when I thought I was losing consciousness and my ridiculous sentence, five hours had passed.

I don't feel any pain and am perfectly wide awake. It's behind me, it's behind me! I repeat to myself with relief.

I am wheeled to my room. Idanna's voice whispers to me very softly, next to my ear:

'He kept the eye. It was not removed.'

NINE

A bandage covers my face from forehead to upper lip. Later, Dr T. comes by to see me. His voice reflects fatigue but I detect something else in it.

'You seem pleased with yourself, Doctor.'

He laughs. The explanations he gives me in his professional voice are too technical for me to understand, but I listen as I try to hear in his voice a little hope, a chance to read my future.

The anaesthetic drugs are gradually wearing off and needles pierce my eyes. Soon two sea urchins have settled in the eye sockets and my brain is on fire. In the middle of the night an ingenious nurse fills two rubber gloves with ice, seals them up tight, and attaches them over my face to act as a decongestant.

In the morning, Idanna laughs as she comes into my room.

'It looks as if a cow's udder has been grafted onto your face!'

The fingers filled with melted ice stick up around my cheeks.

A little later, an intern comes to bring me the report on the operation. A friend who happens to be there reads me the document. Once again, the truth is hidden behind an incomprehensible scientific vocabulary. But there is the last sentence: 'The prognosis for restoring the vision is fair.'

Trumpets sound in the sky; my heart swells with thanksgiving.

'The prognosis for restoring the vision is fair.'

Fair! I cling to that word. As precise and prudent as he is, Dr T. would not have used it without reason. And – considering this surgeon's pessimism – the word leaves no room for uncertainty. I will see again, that's for sure! It's a question of time and fighting.

When Idanna comes back, I tell her the good news and

have her read the prognosis. She doesn't seem to share my enthusiasm or my hope. She even tries to convince me that *fair*, in English, doesn't have any of the optimistic meaning I give it. I am puzzled, disturbed by this reaction. I don't yet know that Michael lied to me and that it isn't *fair* that Idanna is reading with embarrassment, but *poor*. The chances for recovering my vision are *poor*.

I cling to any possible hope. I analyse every word. Each phrase has a meaning. On his next visit, I ask the surgeon questions and he talks to me, in his flat voice, about 'atrophy': 'Perhaps in two years, when a prostho-keratoplasty may partially restore sight in the right eye. It's too early to say.' Definitely, *fair* did not have the meaning I thought it had.

And I think, If in two years, thanks to this prostho-keratoplasty, I can see again, what a shock to be confronted with the world and my friends with that jump in time imprinted on their faces. Similarly, after two years in Asia, I had returned to the café where at one time I used to go every morning to have my coffee and a croissant. The waiter, a good-looking man with a black moustache and laughing eyes, had become a friend. A great ladies' man, he would describe his adventures: 'A saucy little blonde . . . A large coffee, yes, sir! . . . Saucy, there's no other word for her.'

When I sat down at the counter, he had his back to me, doing something with the coffee machine. He turned around, and I was struck by the sight of the face of death. Not that he was sick, far from it, but the light of his eyes was duller, his face had grown fatter, there were lines chiselled in it, you could now see the skin of his skull through his hair. He smiled when he recognised me. I realised that he didn't know he had changed, that every day the finger of death had modified some minute detail. He didn't know, just as someone looking at the hands of a watch doesn't see their movement.

It is very hot and pain doesn't cool me off.

Blind for life, for the rest of my life. What life? Here I am, thrown onto this bed like a fish washed up on the shore. Through the window I hear the flow of life, the hum of New York. I feel how much heavier my body has become from two months of being in bed, making only careful, restricted movements. My neck is stiff and my shoulders tense.

For life . . . what life? I am afraid of rotting away, morally and physically, of giving up.

A blind man returns home on a winter evening, with a big black accordion and his white cane. The place where he lives is poor and lonely. No family, no wife and rosy children. He doesn't turn on the lights and, in the dark, opens a can for his meal. Then he goes to bed and masturbates under the covers to give himself some comfort.

The cliché from the last century's fondness for portrayals of misery. Money, family, love, solitude, these fears, these subjects of anguish are the roars of that monster living down there in darkness.

Lying on that bed, full of fear, I did not yet know that a vital instinct, still intact, was going to give me the strength needed to fight the monster.

This morning, the doctor has come much earlier than usual, around six o'clock.

Breakfast has not yet been served. I am behind with my correspondence and am writing by following the edge of a piece of cardboard I have cut out. To relieve the strain of this demanding task, I have lit up a small Honduran cigar and poured myself a glass of Haitian rum. I hear the doctor's voice:

'Good morning, Monsieur de Montalembert. What are you doing?'

'I am writing, Doctor, just writing.'

My voice sounds perfectly natural, but the truth is that I am extremely embarrassed about the epicurean image I must present at this early-morning hour. Not to mention that alcohol is entirely forbidden in these hallowed halls.

He doesn't say anything, pushes the table aside, and sits down on the bed. I feel his fingers gently lifting up a corner of the bandage on my forehead, and, in a single stroke, he tears my eyes out. No, it can't be, he must have ruined everything the operation has accomplished. The light hurts me.

'I sewed your eyelids together. We can hope that will prevent the eyes from becoming devitalised and then atrophied. The small blood vessels that used to nourish your eyes were burned. Now that your eyelids are kept tightly closed, they are, so to speak, going to graft their blood vessels onto the eyeballs and thus irrigate them. When the upper and lower eyelids have grown together, I'll remove the stitches.'

The bandage relieved the tension by drawing the upper part of my face down and the lower part up. Now that the doctor has removed it, I once again feel needles digging into my eyes, especially the left one. I tell him so and he explains to me:

'The edges of the lids of your left eye were too badly burned to hold the stitches. I had to cut them. That's why you have this feeling of tightness.'

After overwhelming me with scientific details, Dr T. leaves, taking along my glass of Haitian rum, which he probably disapproves of, at least for breakfast.

The telephone rings and I hear the distant voice of my friend Patrick.

'You sound far away.'

'Why? No, not really, Lima.'

'And you are just calling me to say hello?'

'No, but I'm a bit annoyed. I had an appointment with a French engineer and he couldn't take the altitude. It seems he died. No sense of responsibility! Christ Almighty, business is business, regardless of the altitude. You can't count on anybody!'

I laugh. For fifteen years Patrick has been scouring South America with his half-caste looks, though he was born plain and simply in Saint-Loup-du-Dorat, just a few kilometres from the village in Lower Normandy where I myself was born. At the age of seventeen, he rode without stopping across the Mato Grosso, pursued by the fourteen brothers of a young Brazilian woman he had supposedly compromised. He claims he had never been on a horse before.

Some people look down on the telephone. I don't. In this hospital where I am imprisoned in darkness, it brings me space and the possibility of reaching out to others. Telephoning is being able to look through the window. Any distraction is welcome because face to face with myself I am exhausted. I have been cut off from life for days and days. My libido runs amok; erotic images appear all the time. In the middle of a conversation, a vision takes over. The sex of a little girl, swollen, sharply defined with that kind of rounded crescent at the upper end of the opening, hairless. Very beautiful, but disturbing.

Dr George, who owns the Elephant & Castle restaurant, has the manager, Cynthia, bring me dinner every night.

'She has a very beautiful ass and is very lovely,' he tells me confidentially.

I feel like touching her but don't dare to.

I'm afraid, afraid of making others afraid. One evening, while I am having dinner, she sits down on the foot of my bed, unknowingly jostling Aho, who grumbles something to the effect that white men's women don't know how to stay in their place.

'You can't expect her to kneel down and touch her forehead three times on the linoleum like your women in the courtyard dust.'

'That's Africa; you cannot understand. Shut up!'

And he leaves, but he will come back as soon as I call him.

I am aware of the woman's weight on the foot of the bed and the way she smells of sweat and cooking. She has stayed on much longer than usual, no doubt with the complicity of the nurses. I stretch out my hand. She has the robust body of a girl from the Middle West. Her thighs are muscular, her breasts small, with the nipples pointing upward. Her short, strong hair frames a Ukrainian face. Prominent cheekbones, wide eyebrows, turned-up nose, the tenderness of the ear lobe pierced by the cruelty of a gold ring. With the tips of my fingers I lightly touch this feminine puzzle, not always recognising everything. Her ribs thrust forward like the prow of a ship. She assures me she is quite normal. I touch again and try to find her ribs. Her stomach is no longer as flat as a young girl's. She must be over thirty.

Her lips on mine are thick. A strange sensation of kissing

darkness. This abandonment which weighs in my arms. A nurse comes in.

'Ahh! Excuse me, I just wanted to rub your back with alcohol.'
There is laughter in her voice.

'Don't bother,' Cynthia answers. 'I'll take care of it.'

And everybody laughs, except the Jesuit Father behind his curtain, but I wouldn't be surprised if he were smiling.

My head is confused. I feel observed. Each movement she makes catches me by surprise because I cannot predict or stop any of them. I had been afraid of frightening her, but I sense that it is she who is afraid of frightening me. I am relieved when she leaves but there remains the turmoil that has been aroused in me. Something tender is singing.

TEN

'The stitches will be removed in two weeks.'

Three weeks go by, but the left eyelids are too badly burned to grow together and I have to be operated on again.

This time the operation is performed by a woman, Dr Rowland. She has invented a system of clips, which make me suffer less. They have little pieces of sponge attached to them, and once again my face is enclosed by bandages.

Dr T. comes to see me. Always on the lookout for whatever information I can glean from his words, I ask him what comments Dr Rowland had made.

'Everything is all right; it's healing.'

I jump to the conclusion that both eyes are healing, which is much more comforting than what his assistant had responded to the same question an hour earlier:

'Your right eye is doing well and your left eye for the moment is holding.'

Healing . . . Holding. Medical terminology makes every patient suddenly aware of the importance of semantics.

'In a few days you can go home,' the doctor tells me, and slowly my impatience to leave the hospital shifts to indifference – in fact, to hidden fear. Besides, I don't have a home anymore.

A friend leaving for Europe had offered to sublet her apartment to me, but at the last moment she has changed her mind. She admitted later that the idea of my living in her apartment totally confused her. At this stage, nothing surprises me; in any case, my brain has been so washed by the anaesthesias that nothing really registers. Retreating into myself, I analyse my own reactions to get a clue to what lies ahead for me. I have to understand who I am for others, and if the image is distorted, to try to redress it.

'Tomorrow, if you want to, you are free to leave the hospital.'

I have been waiting for this news for several days and now that I am confronted with it I don't know quite how to react. Free! Free to go where? To what future? I consider all the possibilities, but under such conditions no future attracts me. I see a long grey road on which I may advance if courage is there, but what about joy and adventure, the source of all my energy until now? Images cross my mind – I see myself creeping down a street, feeling my way along a wall, dragging my feet.

Horror! I was thirty-five, in the prime of manhood, young and slim, and now I see myself a bloated body, a package of darkness, a crawling locust. I am afraid. I'm afraid to get out, to collect all my courage and still to end up like that.

Admitted on May 25, I am released from the hospital two months later, with six stitches in each eye, blind, handicapped, feeling a nausea for life, for the rest of my life. I do not say this simply to paint a gloomy picture or to make people feel sorry for me; I am trying to explain, as best I can, the fear and mental anguish of those who, like me, have been stabbed in the heart of life.

Officially, I am happy to leave the hospital. I phone some friends to announce the news and to persuade myself that it's a joyful event.

'At long last! Fantastic! You must be glad!'

'Yes . . . Very glad, of course.'

Idanna comes to fetch me, and after saying good-bye to the nurses, we are on the street. My legs feel like cotton and I am already exhausted. The noise of the city engulfs me and encloses my head, the cars seem to be heading right for me. Impossible to get my bearings in this neighbourhood even though I know it by heart down to the smallest detail: Greenwich Avenue, 11th Street, Christopher Street. Geometrical lines and the points of the compass dance in my head. A man passing by shouts to me, 'Watch out for the step!' I stop, holding onto Idanna's arm.

'There is no step,' she says, and I realise how vulnerable I am
to the madness of people who can play such cruel practical jokes.
I recognise the voice; I hear lurking in it the same madness that
threw acid in my face. The animal in me wants to hide deep in
its burrow. Idanna says almost nothing, giving only the directions
for reaching the Elephant & Castle. Again I am confronted with
a sense of shame and injustice towards her. It is so unjust to
impose such suffering upon her; I feel she is wounded, exiled
from the sun. She is trapped. She can't escape without being
condemned. It's unfair since, separated from my life, why should
she share this misfortune? I feel like telling her, 'Leave! This
doesn't concern you, or, rather, I don't want it to concern you.
If people say anything, I'll make them shut up. It isn't drama
that I want to have between us, but something else.'

My bag is heavy in my hand, and it's a relief to put it down on
the floor of the Elephant & Castle. The room is cool and filled
with Cynthia's smell, which is the smell of the kitchen. A cup of
coffee, a piece of cheesecake; I kiss all the waitresses Cynthia
introduces to me. We laugh, exchange jokes, but actually my
brain is wooden; I act and talk like a robot, with apparent good
humour, but underneath it all, I only wish I could jump back into
my hospital bed.
    Later, I put my bag down in the apartment that has been
sublet for me, the layout of which I don't understand. There I
meet Désirée, a Haitian who will take care of me. Idanna takes
me to a Japanese restaurant on the West Side. I am worn out
but pretend not to be because already, instinctively, I am fighting
off a sort of torpor. Idanna is a good ally, because she isn't prone
to pity and her confidence in my abilities forces me to do my
utmost. It is Friday night, the restaurant is full, the waiter is
Japanese and homosexual, the voice tells me everything. Sounds
pour into my head indiscriminately. To follow the conversation
across the table is impossible. Idanna is absorbed in a discussion
with a friend who has joined us. She has a ticket for Honolulu in
her pocket and confesses to me how happy she is 'to throw
myself into the arms of the sea.' Behind me, a woman says,
'Delicious!' and a man's drunken voice snaps back, 'Delicious!

Delicious! You haven't even tasted it! The goddam trouble with you is that everything is always delicious. It's not delicious; it's lousy!' I don't know why I hear these words more clearly than the ones directed at me, but very quickly they also sink into a chaos of laughter, clattering dishes, and the rumble of general conversation. I listen, gaping. I don't see them but I have the impression that it is they who don't see me.

ELEVEN

My body feels soft, my joints stiff. Put a stop to this deterioration, phone the rehabilitation centre that promised to accept me quickly but that I haven't heard from.

'Hello. Lighthouse. Good afternoon!'

I explain, I request; they switch me from one department to another.

'We'll send someone in a few days to evaluate you.'

Three days later, Mrs Finklestein, an instructor in Mobility and Orientation, rings my doorbell. She has brought a folding cane, and we go down to the street.

'Try to walk on your own.'

The fracas of the two-way traffic on 86th Street makes my head swim and, instinctively, I walk towards the buildings to escape danger. 'Good Lord, how can anyone walk alone without being able to see?' I'm afraid of the noises, cars, holes, and lampposts.

'Take my arm.'

We walk. I hear the row of buildings come to an end. My head is struck so brutally by the sun that I float in the light. We have just left the shadow of 86th Street. I have completely lost my sense of direction. Through my stitched eyelids, I see. It may not be much, but when I see the shadow of my hand between the sun and myself, I experience equally the pleasure and the absurdity of the situation. I feel that between the world and me there is nothing more than a thin piece of cigarette paper and that it would take very little to tear it.

I listen to the vast canyon of Madison Avenue.

'Where are we?' she asks me as a test.

'On the northeast corner of Madison and 86th.'

'No. We're on the southwest corner of Park Avenue and 86th.'

I don't understand and think back over the way we came. I had simply assumed that my apartment building was on the north side of the street, but it's on the south side. It will take several weeks to erase this mistake from my brain, in fact I think I never got rid of it completely. And that's how I became aware of something that will happen often. When it comes to orientations, every clue is printed in indelible characters on my memory. This is an advantage in that I am able to register a place, a house, an apartment, an itinerary once and for all. I can return much later and find my direction without thinking. On the other hand, if I absent-mindedly make a mistake, I go on repeating the same mistake endlessly.

'What hints might have helped you realise you were wrong?'

It's like a game; I feel my brain get stimulated.

'I hear that this avenue is much larger than Madison and that there is traffic in both directions, while Madison is one-way.'

'Could you tell me what colour the traffic lights are?'

Easy! I listen carefully. The stream of cars flows in front of me and comes to a stop, then the cars on my left start up and go east on 86th Street.

'Red light on Park Avenue, green on 86th Street.'

We wait for the lights to change some more, and I follow them without any trouble.

'That way you will be able to choose the right moment to cross the street. We are going around the block. Where are we?'

'Northeast corner of 85th and Madison.'

'Lean on the sound of the traffic line. That is the clue you will have to use to walk straight.'

I listen but I don't understand how this chaotic noise will help me walk straight. Far from being a line, the noise strikes me as being a huge ink blot, and besides, all I want to do now is to go home to the silence of my apartment, to exchange Mrs Finklestein's professional voice for Désirée's Creole one.

'You should be able to learn quickly,' she said. 'You have a good sense of orientation and observation. The next session begins in October. There's a waiting list, but I will recommend that they take you right away.'

This first experience with the possibility of moving about without having to ask anyone for anything thrills me, makes my heart beat faster, erases my fatigue and the stagnation of my brain. The fact is that I have understood the game. I interpret clearly the information provided by sounds and transform them into spatial terms, height, width, parallel and perpendicular lines, movement and direction. But I don't quite understand what Mrs Finklestein meant by 'to walk straight you should lean on the sound of the traffic line.' However hard I listened, I couldn't trace that line. And yet I am helped by the fact that I had been intensely, passionately visual, that I had studied drawing and perspective and had learned to organise space in painting pictures.

Once back in the apartment, Mrs Finklestein shows me how to use the aluminium cane she has brought. I try it out by walking around the various rooms, giving the furniture vigorous taps, discovering unknown corners, a fireplace in the living room, a Spanish-something-or-other baroque cabinet.

Now I have a better visual idea of the place I am living in. In my enthusiasm I decide to go and visit Claire, a friend who lives three floors below me. I close the front door, leaving Désirée flabbergasted. The elevator comes; I get into it quickly and put my hand where I know the buttons are, but my fingers encounter something that has nothing to do with what I had expected. After three seconds of groping, reality dawns, rather embarrassingly. It is a nose, and yet there is no reaction. I burst out laughing, which prevents me from making the appropriate apologies, and we reach the ground floor without any other form of communication. The elevator's automatic door opens and a woman's footsteps walk away. I ask the doorman who it was.

'Mrs Simpson, on the sixth floor.'

Every day I make a point of going throughout the apartment without touching the walls, without bumping into the furniture. An armchair in the middle of the hallway? How could that be?

Maybe Désirée moved it when she was cleaning and forgot to push it back. I go around it and run into a bookcase I didn't know about. I grope along; walls surround me; I retrace my steps and encounter another wall. I am boxed in a space with no exit. It does not help me to turn in every direction, for I encounter pieces of furniture, curtains, bibelots that my fingers knock over, but I find no door. It's enough to make me wonder what looking glass I have stepped through. Some kind of animal instinct makes my heart beat like crazy, but it is not panic, since I have nothing to fear. A telephone rings. So I am in the study. The sound tells me where it is. A voice pronounces the name of the people from whom I have sublet the apartment. I give the appropriate information and hang up. I know where the door is in relation to the desk in the middle of the room and go out into the hallway with no problem. I have just experienced one of the major problems I will have to learn to cope with – my unfortunate tendency to veer to the left. Unwittingly, I went through the door of the study at an angle. If this kind of mistake can happen in such a restricted and familiar space, I realise that walks in Central Park are not for tomorrow.

Every day I try to while away the time before crashing into bed. I've got to find things to keep myself busy: make up my telephone book on tape because Désirée doesn't know how to read and can only spell names out slowly; do my correspondence, which wears me out quickly; record tapes for my family in France.

Every afternoon, when I collapse, all I can do is observe how little I have accomplished, what small progress I have made. Every morning I wake up between four and five, full of energy, optimism, and appetite for the day that is about to begin; every evening there is the feeling of defeat. Day after day I am defeated. Stretched out on my bed, with nothing to do, I 'make television'. My brain produces images, films, stories coming from unknown sources. It is a drug, a necessary escape. I must continue to create images, to visualise my surroundings. Dr T. had warned me, 'The brain cells that control vision run the risk of becoming atrophied.'

Thanks to my insomnia, I discover radio programmes of a

very special kind that play only at night. Just a studio with telephones. Sometimes the broadcast has a theme, and all around there are people listening in New York City and the entire metropolitan area, New Jersey, and Connecticut. Anyone who wants to can call in. Everything is anonymous; people can make their confessions without being identified. One night the theme is cruising. In answer to the question 'What is your best asset?' the women as well as the men respond 'Eyes.' What I hear is also their solitude, which they may be able to escape from by looking into others' eyes. 'Chance led our eyes to meet, and I may know you.' This almost accidental form of communication is now forbidden to me. Such encounters will never occur, but I already know that, for the very same reason, others have taken place.

For hours Désirée remains seated, without moving, facing my bed. She does nothing; she just watches me. I am aware of her stare, but I've given up telling her she can go out or do whatever she has to do for herself. She says 'Yes' and doesn't move.

One morning she declares, 'We must buy a cabaret.' I agree, slightly taken aback. A cabaret! I have considered lots of solutions for the future, but not running a cabaret. After hearing long explanations in a mixture of French and Creole, I finally understand that a 'cabaret' is a tray like the one we use for breakfast, which she considers too small.

Désirée always walks around barefoot, the African way. The first morning she put this breakfast tray on my bed without making the slightest sound. As a result, I sat on the coffeepot and burned my bottom. To cool off, I went in to have a bath, and in the silence of that peaceful retreat I was deep in thought. Suddenly I let out a shout: a hand had grabbed my leg. Without saying a word, Désirée was soaping me just as she no doubt scours her sink, quietly and carefully.

Désirée doesn't say much. Désirée is sad because she is thinking about her six children at her mother-in-law's, far off in the mountains of Haiti. Désirée is sad because she is thinking about the slut who took her husband away from her. 'It's not his fault; he is weak.' She loves him, that much I can hear in her heartbroken voice.

In this apartment I have sublet from some Brazilians who are away on holiday, I have discovered a pile of samba records. Samba! Let's samba, Désirée! And here we are dancing. I can hear the floor creaking rhythmically as she swings to the music. Samba! To hell with Anglo-Saxon nurses! I interviewed one with lavender hair whose prim voice announced, 'I am used to handicapped people.'

Samba, Désirée! Let's forget about your lonely children and the stinking liquid oozing from my eyes. But my head starts spinning very soon and not seeing the floor makes me dizzy.

Far, far away are the nights at the Cosmos, in Cotonou, Dahomey, dancing all night, Lupa-Lupa band, Zairois or Nigerian singers, the smell of overheated bodies. Dubious girls who look at you like princesses, dancing with the music, never with you, to proclaim their independence. Young street boys dressed to kill, with a pimplike indifference, dark glasses and high heels and not the vaguest prospect of a job.

TWELVE

In October, through one of those chance happenings that occur only in New York, a businessman I don't know lets me use his suite at the Carlyle.

So it is in front of that grand hotel that a taxi picks me up to take me to the rehabilitation centre, the Lighthouse, on 59th Street. It is nine o'clock. The lobby reverberates with strident voices. As I was soon to learn, blind people use their voices not only to communicate with the person they are talking to but also to announce their presence to some blind friend who might be passing by. This is known as their 'broadcasting voice.'

The atmosphere is not sad, but all the same, my stomach is in knots. There is a strained air in this lobby. A kind of tension. In an absurd way it seems to me that violence may break out at any moment. Canes click against one another. Fencing, fencing to avoid contact. This noise is dreadful to my ears. Dogs shake their harnesses. They never bark except for a brief yelp when a blind person steps on their paw. In the background I hear the switchboard operators' voices:

'Good morning, Lighthouse.'

The taxi driver has dropped me off here and left without a word. I don't know what to do, I am being pushed about, I feel unsteady on my feet. This constant vertigo. I feel the same as when I first went away to school, full of expectations, longing to get the hell out of there, and absolutely convinced that I had to stay. Nausea rises in my throat. . . . Just as at school, I feel that I don't belong, that I don't want to belong. I listen to the nice things said to me as if each represented a danger. The voice of an instructor:

'Good morning, sweetheart! How handsome you look this

morning!' I hear her voice repeating exactly the same words in exactly the same tone a little farther on. Shame!

The loss of my eyes forces me to begin a new kind of education without the help of a family, of a mother or father, but with the aid of institutions that are more concerned with efficiency than love. Social workers take me in hand. In such a process, love is even discouraged; it could only impede this business of rehabilitation. The instructors' frustration, the anger and violence of the instructed are a palpable presence in this building, like a sinister fog.

'Hello, Monsieur de Montalembert! I am Judy Axelrod. I'm a volunteer and will guide you on this first day. Take my arm, please.'

The elevator is full; hands brush against one another. A woman laughs idiotically. I discover later that there are special programmes for the blind who are mentally ill.

From time to time a recorded voice announces: 'Second floor. Please push button for the floor you desire.'

I have no desire for any floor, and what's more, I don't know where I am going. Fifth floor. We turn right and go into a small smoke-filled room. I am taken to an armchair. There are eight of us around a table, five blind men and three blind women. An instructor asks us to introduce ourselves to one another, briefly. One man refuses to speak, to give so much as his name. At the other extreme, at eighty-two years of age, a real black mama launches into a rhythmical account, with endless humorous details, of her recent life as a blind woman, and winds up by saying, 'Never mind. Thank God it doesn't really matter to me, because all my children are in good health and they make enough money to help me out.'

When my turn comes, I simply say, 'My name is Hugues. I am French and have been blind for five months. Accident.'

The director of the Department of Rehabilitation gives a talk about the choices available to us. A blind lawyer briefs us on blind people's rights: reductions on bus fares, postage, food stamps in certain cases, the right to keep your faithful dog next to you in public places. I can almost feel a begging bowl growing in my hand. Then come explanations of taxes and welfare rights, which don't concern me, because I'm not American. I am quite aware of the fact that there is no window in the room and that bothers me a little; I am bothered by this whole new windowless world. Blind laws, blind building, blind companions. I want a world with windows.

Judy Axelrod takes me to have lunch in the cafeteria. One tray knocks against the next as they are moved along the counter. There is a crowd and the room is particularly noisy because of the habit the blind have of broadcasting their presence. In one corner, bizarre sounds, high-pitched laughs – the mental patients, the ones who spend several years acquiring the sense of up and down, over and under, horizontal and vertical. I listen to this hellish sound of the damned.

After lunch, I go to see the man in charge of arranging my schedule. He's a nice fellow who uses a paternalistic approach to cover up for not being able to make out who I am. Born and married in a Jewish community in Brooklyn where he has lived for forty-eight years, he treats me as if I were an Indian from Patagonia.

'So, Monsieur de Montalembert, since I read in your file that you painted, I have signed you up for the pottery and sculpture studio.'

He takes this for granted, but it leaves me dumbfounded.

Mr Scholtz has taken courses in psychology that have qualified him for this position, and I will discover that actually he's right. It works in almost every case: you were a photographer, so I signed you up for pottery.

'Do you know many great sculptors who are blind?'

'What do you mean? There are no great sculptors who are blind. No such thing exists. You can mess around with clay and have a good time, but that's all.'

'Painting was much more for me than just having a good time.'

'You're wrong. A very, very good show of paintings by blind artists has just opened at the Metropolitan Museum.'

'Yes, I know, probably three floors below ground level. It

would be more honest to have them exhibit in a circus. Sign me up for piano.'

'Fine! I didn't know you were a musician.'

'I haven't ever been one but I feel like beginning. I see more possibilities along that line than in the visual arts. With music, at least I can hear my wrong notes. For me, painting and sculpture are much too serious to play around with; I'd only be frustrated. Music is new and won't remind me of anything.'

'How interesting! I hadn't looked at the question from that angle. So I'll sign you up for a one-hour piano lesson and three hours of practice every week. And what about other activities?'

'Braille, typing – since I don't know how to type without looking at the keys – cooking and housekeeping. I just want to be able to live alone and independently, in case I have to. For instance, being able to sew on a button.'

Mr Scholtz smells of sweat.

'That's very good; you know what you want and that's very encouraging.'

I am tempted to stick out my hand to receive my gold stars.

'Still, let me recommend our classes in communications. You will learn how to use the library; the publications are in Braille and some are on flexible discs. Ah, yes, there is also Miss Wallenstein, who referred you here after talking to you in the hospital. She would like to see you once a week. And then there is our Recreation Department.'

'No. I'll get my recreation outside. But OK for communications and Miss Wallenstein.'

'We have bowling.'

'That's even worse than sculpture!'

He decides to laugh. I am the Indian from Patagonia. But, in spite of it, I remained on excellent terms with him. He is basically very good-hearted, though completely devoid of a sense of humour. He lets me get by with all sorts of irregularities, especially my prolonged and repeated absences when I just can't bear to go on facing the same old routine, and my shipwrecked hopes.

*   *   *

A little later, a woman explains some highly sophisticated machines to me by going through a memorised speech. Points press into the palm of my hand. According to their position, they correspond to the letters of a book placed in front of an electronic eye. But one machine is particularly admirable. She puts a book in it and a disembodied, jerky, uninflected voice reads: 'The birds soared off over the sun-drenched field of wheat and . . . please turn the page.'

I burst out laughing.

'I don't see what's so funny,' she says in a rather huffy tone of voice.

Embarrassed, I apologise and try to explain:

'No, no. I was just imagining a love story, even something erotic, read that way. In any case, it can be very useful.'

In any case, the machine costs six thousand dollars and for that amount you can hire someone who, in addition to reading with feeling and a variety of intonations, would be able to turn the pages herself.

All the machines that this technician shows me – talking calculators, among others – are well beyond my means and the means of the blind in general. So, after tempting me with her electronic voice, the woman packs up her stock and disappears.

She has left me alone in this room, rather happy to be by myself for a few moments. The building is relatively silent. Voices can be heard in offices, behind closed doors, and the bell of the elevator stopping at this floor, high-pitched to indicate that it's going up, low-pitched that it's going down. The doors slide automatically and the trained tenor voice announces 'Fifth floor' and the doors close again. Silence. Then timidly, hesitantly, here and there the tapping of a cane on the floor in the corridor; the tapping becomes regular, the blind person has located the wall and is following it with his cane.

Tap . . . tap . . . tap . . . tap . . . tap . . . This noise is inhuman. I hear the hesitations. I wonder what goes on in that mind. What is he or she heading for? It is impossible, when you hear this tapping, not to feel the solitude. All that courage to arrive where? The blind person turns around and comes back, approaches, finds the door of the room I'm in, and enters.

'Hello!' He must have smelled the smoke of my cigarette. 'Who are you? I'm Jack.'

He has a deep, musical voice. He sits down; we talk. He's in his fifties. As a truck driver, he spent twenty years on the road, back and forth, coast to coast. He gradually lost the sight of one eye, said nothing, and went on driving his truck. He explains this simply, very calmly. Then a year ago, the other eye began to deteriorate. 'It was just as well. Driving with one eye wore me out so much that I would have had an accident eventually. And I managed to work until my kids were off on their own.' God be praised!

'And now?'

'Oh, now I just stay home. My wife is glad to have me pretty much to herself.'

'Do you read?'

'Only one book! Because I find all the other books in that one. It's a book about love, philosophy, poetry, a detective thriller, an adventure story.'

'Really? What's the name of this book?'

'The Bible!'

Not an ordinary truck driver. He told me that in exactly the same way he would have said how much pressure to put in his tyres. Jack was one of the rare serene blind people I met at the rehabilitation centre.

It is five o'clock and I am exhausted.

In the lobby, Désirée's hand grasps my arm, and I tell her impatiently:

'Viens!'

Behind me I hear a woman's voice. 'All my life I've waited for someone to say to me "Viens!" – with the voice of Charles Boyer.'

I turn around. It is the switchboard operator.

'Why did you say "with the voice of Charles Boyer"?'

'Because, darling, it's a horizontal voice.'

At last, I make my way into the lobby of the Carlyle. It is the last of today's efforts. Conversations stop and I am clearly the centre of attention as I move through the silence. Désirée

creates a sensation with her flowery hat. It is a relief to hear
the door of the apartment closing behind me.

The suite at the Carlyle, soundproofed, thickly carpeted,
luxurious, provides a welcome contrast to the functional, chilly
environment of the Lighthouse, with those strange voices in
the corridors, that tapping of aluminium canes, those sweaty
smells.

Sitting cross-legged on the carpet in the living room, Désirée is
picking over spinach leaves, busily thinking about her children.
From the kitchen float the smells of Haitian cooking. I am not
hungry, too tired, too tense. A warm bath helps my muscles
relax. Lying still in the water, adjusting the faucets with my feet
to control the temperature, I reflect. It's going to be tough! I
don't like the Lighthouse, but the people there have everything
I need, and if I use it to the maximum, I can soon be free again.
My eyes hurt. How is it that the stitches haven't yet been
removed? Dr T. examines me every week. Apparently, my
eyelids are not growing together. I am going to need a lot of
patience. The question that keeps coming back over and over
again in my head about this rehabilitation is: How long will it
take? I asked Mr Scholtz about it.

'Oh, that varies from case to case. You can't make any
predictions.'

'I understand, but still, for the average blind person, how
much time does it take?'

'Well, you see, that depends on his aspirations, or you might
say his ambitions.'

Rubbish. It's clear that they don't want to give me an answer.
Page 36 of the Teacher's Manual: 'Do not set time limits. The
clients may run into some difficulty and become discouraged.'
And so I go through this rehabilitation at a brisk pace but under
the impression that I am slow and not very gifted. Having no
frame of reference and being impatient and proud by nature, I
soon reach the point of nervous exhaustion. When tingling
sensations in my fingertips prevent me from reading Braille, I
am convinced it is gout or something wrong with my heart or
my circulation. 'You're going at it too fast. You must ease up.

Your nerves are frazzled. Take it easy, slow down, relax,' the instructors keep repeating.

But an impulsiveness drives me to the breaking point. Then, unreasonably, I reject the Lighthouse. I play hooky, sometimes for as long as a week. Interruptions included, I used the rehabilitation centre for about ten months.

Mobility turned out to be a real challenge, the most fascinating and sometimes the most depressing one. Straight lines were never my forte, as was obvious from my life style, and now I discover that I don't even walk straight. The first time I realised this was outside, at my friend Claire's place in the country.

I wake up as usual around five o'clock and listen to the birds through the open window. I had forgotten, perhaps I have never listened to them so intently. Perhaps I have never expected so much from birds. Through my eyelids, the morning sun casts a glow upon my brain. I feel full of joy and confidence.

Reassured by the surroundings – I was, after all, born in the country – I dare to go outside alone for the first time. And I decide to go by the swimming pool and listen to the news on my little radio. I am interested in the election of the Pope and admire a political system, neither a democracy nor a dictatorship, that handles so smoothly the death of two popes within a matter of days.

The house is asleep. I open the door. My hand brushes a bush. It is wet with dew. I recognise beneath my fingers the little round, hard leaf; I crush it between my thumb and forefinger, and the smell of box fills the air. I walk around the clumps of bushes with the help of the cane Mrs Finklestein gave me. There is a contrast between the dry air of the house and the damp, dewy atmosphere outdoors. The filter motor is humming and, guided by this sound, I reach the swimming pool. I go around it, to find the armchair I want to sit in. I put the radio down on a table, draw up the chair, and fall into the pool. Shades of Charlie Chaplin!

I decide to go in to change my dripping clothes. The house is a hundred yards away. With my cane I imprint on my brain the edge of the pool and from there follow a perpendicular line that will take me to the house. I don't find the house. A hundred yards isn't far, but being ten degrees off produces an error that is wider than a house. A matter of simple geometry . . .

I try again ten times, and ten times I miss the house. My morale, which hasn't been affected by falling into the pool – actually, that made me laugh – begins to crumble. The sun is warmer and I am sweating in spite of my wet clothes, more from impatience than from the heat. At the beginning I scold myself: 'To miss a house, really!' Fortunately, the filter motor hums along calmly and it is easy for me to go back to where I started. I set off along the same perpendicular line, moving steadily forward. But nothing. The house has disappeared. I listen, trying to hear its presence. Nothing. It's not a game anymore, and my stomach sinks. I am so enraged that I don't even go back to the edge of the pool to get my bearings. I tap against the bushes, run into the trees, get lost and completely disorientated. I sit down on the grass and force my heart to calm down.

The birds are still singing and the sun-warmed leaves give off their scent. A plan takes shape in my head. Once again, I aim at the motor. I am surprised to reach the pool on a completely different side from the one I had arbitrarily expected.

I realign myself according to the edge that I know is opposite the house, then count off a hundred steps and breathe slowly through my nose. The sweetish, somewhat bitter smell of box fills my nostrils. The sun evaporating the dew has turned the bushes into incense. The smell comes from the right. I let my nose guide me and reach the door without difficulty.

I climb the stairs to my room, take off my clothes, already dried by the sun, and rest on the bed. My legs are trembling from nervous exhaustion.

A little later, the house has woken up. I go down to the kitchen and sit at the breakfast table. 'A Polish pope has been elected,' I announce. That's a scoop, but while comments are being made about it, my thoughts are elsewhere. A secret life, incommunicable and impossible to share.

THIRTEEN

Since I have been staying at the Carlyle, Désirée leaves every evening to go sleep at her brother-in-law's in Brooklyn.

When the thick hotel door closes and I face my first night alone, I stand with my feet deep in the carpet for a long time without moving, leaning my forehead against the wall, listening to the mounting panic. Panic against which the force of all my will can only erect a fragile barrier. I feel that the slightest movement of my body could break the dike and that this thing which I don't even want to define would surge up in me like thirty thousand galloping Barbarians, leaving me devastated. I hear the sounds of my body perfectly, the way I swallow, the circulation of life. Then, little by little, the sounds of the city through the window, the sirens at the nearby hospital, all that New York violence which used to fascinate me, like being given permission to visit hell.

What meaning am I to find in what has happened to me? This question obsesses me. If there is no meaning in it, then it is terrible, because there is no worse punishment. Such agony, a twenty-four-hour-a-day struggle to overcome fear. My courage puzzles me but it is not mine; it is the courage of this living species, the human being. There is a force in me that does not belong to me but that is everybody's; in the same way my weakness, my neuroses, and my weariness do not belong to me, nor does my despair, which is never very far off. Sometimes, I don't even know if I am pretending to be what I am or if that is what I really am.

Some people find a meaning in what has happened to me. A teacher of transcendental meditation who teaches in a factory tells me:

'It is a blessing from God!'

'No! Don't insult God.'

I squeeze my cane, which I feel like breaking on his head.

In a lecture at the Lighthouse, someone who lost his sight in an accident declares, 'Since I've been blind, I have become a much better person.'

'Cut off your legs; you'll be even better!' I shout to him from my seat.

A blind Hindu who recently arrived here from Bombay is the only one who laughs. The others think I have problems. I leave the lecture with Jet, the Hindu.

Among the blind there is probably a temptation to believe that their condition automatically puts them on a higher spiritual plane. Very often the people around them encourage it. Sincerely, I refuse to go along with this farce. Priests talk to me and I hear in their voices a kind of complicity that they take for granted, something to do with the suffering of Jesus on the cross, our shared crucifixion. I am not there and would like it to be known that I am not. True to what Aho taught me, I don't want to lose contact with my own reality. Loss of sight is a mechanical accident, not a state of grace or an event fraught with spiritual consequences.

Deep down, I suspect that all this has no meaning. The thought grows little by little, and both soothes and torments me. You cannot suddenly become an atheist after centuries of belief and a whole childhood of indoctrination without feeling insecure and excluded. I know it can sever me from my mother's love and make me be rejected by my tribe. Man does not like to be alone. He feels stronger in a group. And I am afraid, like everybody else, of nights out on the steppes, without the shelter of a roof and a hearth.

In this overly plush hotel room, such thoughts keep coming back, and they are corroborated later by my father when he tells me:

'I am sad because I think that after my death I will never see some of my children again.'

What does he mean by 'some'?

'I mean that some of them won't go to heaven.'

Sometimes my soul feels heavy with the weight of my inheritance and I need other people desperately to keep up my courage. Alone, I cannot do anything. If I lose my tribe, I must find another. Man cannot wander around alone, without a home and a woman to sleep with.

The telephone is sitting there on the Louis Quinze desk. I go over to touch it, to examine its possibilities. I try to imagine its ring and immediately I feel tense with expectation. I cannot make a call myself, for I'm much too afraid of provoking pity. Later, I will reach a stage where even that barrier disappears and pride doesn't exist anymore. If the telephone doesn't ring, I'm going to scream! I imagine my voice answering. Will the other person, listening, perceive my fear?

Hello! My voice sounds strange, muffled by the carpeting and the curtains. I force myself to move about, turn on the television, go into the bedroom. The bed is wider than it is long; there is a grotesque dressing table with a gauze skirt. In the bathroom, a telephone next to the basin. A tiny kitchen where no one has ever done any cooking.

A key turns in the lock. Two chambermaids come in. They go into the bedroom, into the bathroom. I hope they are going to talk to me, but they leave, saying only:

'Good night.'

'Thank you,' I answer.

It's the end of their working day. They are in a hurry. They are going to go back home, to their loved ones.

'Good night.' The door closes behind them.

I give the sofa pillow a punch. React, for God's sake!

But there's nothing to be done. I am sunk, my throat is tight, and here I am crying like an idiot, without a sound. It is eight o'clock, the restaurants are full, the lights are going down in Carnegie Hall and the curtain is going up at the Metropolitan Opera. The cafés in SoHo are swarming with people. It is 8:00 P.M.; New Yorkers entertain themselves after the most colossal working day in the world. It's time for ladies to sparkle. October ushers in the cultural season: concert halls, galleries, theatres. A new wind is blowing over the city.

Do something, for God's sake! Tonight Bobby Short is playing the piano at the bar seven floors below me. Ring! Someone from the hotel will take you there and maybe, by pretending to have a good time, you will have a good time. Get away, whatever it takes! Get away from being alone with yourself. No, you've got to see this thing through to the end. Then, if you don't go crazy, you can dig yourself out of the sand and leave this shore.

There are all kinds of guests in this hotel, even though it is said to be the most aristocratic in New York.

One morning when I come back after a walk in Central Park, two men in the elevator are laughing so hard at each other's jokes that I think they are going to fall over. I can imagine the look of Désirée's raised eyebrows beneath the brim of her hat. When they leave, Bill the elevator man says:

'That's Mr Jack Nicholson and Mr Dustin Hoffman. They're supposed to be writing a screenplay together, but it doesn't look as if they're in very great shape this morning. And it seems that they don't wash anymore.'

It's true that they have left an acrid smell behind them.

On another day, we have the honour of sharing an elevator with Mick Jagger. Not a word. It is eight in the morning. Wearing a crimson velvet jacket, the rock star is going to bed. Bill, who is getting more and more familiar, says:

'That was Mr Mick Jagger,' and then, lowering his voice, 'a really arrogant son of a bitch.'

Brushing up against high society doesn't impress Désirée. To tell the truth, she seems to be completely indifferent. I find it entertaining. I go down to the bar. I listen to people's conversations, which are in every conceivable language. Iranian women complain about not finding servants in New York. There are also Nicaraguan women who have the same problems but in Spanish, and they talk about their nation's ingratitude towards Somoza. There are Arab conversations, solely male. There are Texans who talk too loud. Clinking of chains and bracelets. The women's perfumes mix with the smell of martinis and cigars.

*   *   *

Little by little I discover that it is easier for me to communicate with women simply because it is not easy for men to touch each other. Women feel no hesitation about punctuating their words with very specific gestures. When I am sitting down, they first touch my knees, which are neutral territory, then my forearms, and finally my hands.

I force myself to go out. The first time I experience what it is like to be blind in the middle of a crowd is at a farewell cocktail party for a journalist friend of mine. After a few minutes, deafened, I sit down on a sofa. There is a woman on my right. She begins to ask me questions, touch my knees, squeeze my forearms, press my hands, drop her lighter and pick it up between my legs; the result is that I start to feel slightly aroused. A doubt flashes through my mind: She must be quite ugly and think she has a chance with me.

When she finally leaves me to get drinks, I quickly ask a man I feel to be on my left:

'Excuse me, this woman I was talking to, how does she look?'

'She is the most beautiful woman in the room!'

Just then I hear her voice:

'I see you have met my husband!'

And then there's this Frenchman who introduces himself:

'We don't know each other, but I have heard about you from . . .'

'We know each other very well. Fourteen years ago we were together at the university.'

He expresses surprise, seems to remember, then introduces his wife to me, for some reason using her maiden name. She also says:

'We don't know each other, but I have heard about you. . . .'

'We know each other very well. We danced together fifteen years ago.'

And both exclaim:

'What a memory you have!'

'Not at all, but I'm very good at remembering faces.'

*   *   *

Turning too quickly from the hallway into my bedroom, I bumped into the doorframe. The ridge of my brow is split open. I am obsessed by the idea that something may penetrate my eye sockets, which aren't defended by my sight. These two holes are points of extreme vulnerability in my body, through which something might pierce me right through to my brain. To make up for not having my sight as a defence, I have a band in the shape of glasses cut out of a sheet of steel. The metal reflects the lights of the city, other people's eyes, like mirrors used to catch larks. It covers my fear, my wound, with a kind of brutal arrogance. This band rules out pity.

My shins are black and blue from bumping against the coffee table in the living room, armchairs, or the foot of the bed. I must learn how to slow down and move around more carefully. The Jamaican chambermaids who observe me suggest pushing the table against the wall. I absolutely refuse. Better to learn how to adapt myself to the world as it is, rather than to adapt the world to my situation.

One morning, while taking a shower, I drop the soap and, absent-mindedly, bend over to pick it up. One of the wall faucets hits my left eye, the more fragile one. Two stitches give way. Dr T., whom I go to see right away, tells me that the eye is all right but that, in any case, another operation is needed because my eyelids refuse to grow together. The badly burned edge has to be cut again and new stitches must be put in. What bothers me is having to undergo another general anaesthesia. Head operations require very special anaesthesia. I come out of it fatigued, empty, as if my brain had been scrubbed.

In my room at the hospital I find a man who had his brow ridge and nose broken when he was punched right in the face by an unknown passer-by.

'I live in New Jersey,' he said, 'but every year for our wedding anniversary my wife and I go dancing in a club on Sixth Avenue. Oh, no big deal; it's just a little joint that has good music. And can you believe it! We leave the place around midnight and that guy smashes my face in right there outside the club and leaves. Shit! He didn't even stop. And nobody tried to stop him, either.'

'Hard luck.'

'Not at all. Just the opposite! The three weeks I've spent here have been the best of my life. The nurses have been taking wonderful care of me; they pamper me and everybody has left me in peace. You see, for thirty-eight years I worked in a bank. Oh, I wasn't a director or executive. No, just an ordinary clerk. Then it was time to retire. The kids were off on their own and I was bored stiff around the house. The fucking house, the fucking dog, and the fucking wife! We decided to tour Europe, especially Italy, because my wife was taking art classes. Shit! I was just about the only male in the bunch, it was mainly women crazy about Art, most of them spending their poor dead husband's money. Venice for drawing, Rome for sculpture, Siena for painting. In Florence I slipped away, it was going to be architecture. I rented a place by myself in a little boardinghouse. A room with a balcony. So I sat out on the balcony and did what I had never had the time to do, I watched how people live.

'In the room next to mine there was a Danish woman, a beautiful blonde, a veterinarian. I had never cheated on my wife, had never even thought of it, but there I was, sixty years old and sleeping with the veterinarian. Do you think I felt guilty? Not a bit! Shit! I felt fantastically alive. I didn't say anything to my wife but I decided to take a month's vacation alone every year. To hell with the fucking house, the fucking wife, and the fucking dog. This year I'll go to Spain, to the Costa Brava, and I'll find a little room with a balcony. And if there's a blonde lady in the room next to mine, fine!'

Later in the afternoon, his wife came in to get him. It was his last day in the hospital.

'Hello, hello, darling. How glad you must be to go home at last! If you could see the dog! He is jumping all over; he knows you're coming home today. I've fixed a special Welcome Home dinner.'

Her voice is shrill, artificial, like the colour of her hair, no doubt. She is nothing more than one of the molecules which constitute that immense American middle class. She may belong to the silent majority, but that description scarcely applies to

her, and the guy says to me, in a whisper, 'See what I mean?'
And rather sadly he goes off.

I was operated on yesterday. It was a minor operation but one
that nonetheless took quite a while because of its precision. I
have new stitches and have almost no pain, just a certain
tightness. My brain is working and doesn't seem to be so washed
out. So I decide to go home and I get my things together. The
nurses try to tell me that I can't leave without the doctor's
authorisation, but, unlike my neighbour, I have had as much of
the hospital as I can take.

'Just tell the doctor I'll see him in his consulting room.'

My mother, paralysed with arthritis of the hip, has not been
able to come to see me. So I must go to her and relieve the
grief I sense in the letters she records on tape. Sometimes I
don't have enough courage to listen to them, and wait for several
days before putting them into my tape recorder. Her voice
sounds heartbroken as she tells me about minor family happenings, and she always ends up by advising me to turn to the
Blessed Virgin Mary, even though she knows how sceptical I
am. She asks me questions, but her voice drops at the end of
the sentence instead of rising into an interrogative tone. She
isn't really asking for an answer, because she is obsessed by
another question, one that she can't formulate and that I can't
make out. I am instinctively afraid of the questions lurking in
the silences of the tape. It is as if they had an unspoken reproach.
I know that to her my hectic life makes me the guilty party as
well as the victim. Judeo-Christian morality doesn't recognise
chance. I may well project my own guilt into my mother's
silence, for who wants to be a source of sorrow for someone he
loves? It is not my mission to be a redeemer and so I have no
good reason to plunge a dagger into my mother's heart, like the
images of the Virgin in the village church.

Discovering Tuscany through my marriage, I noticed that
there were two kinds of Pietà: those in which the Mother of the
Creator, overwhelmed with sorrow, looks at her Son and says
to him, 'What have you done to me!' and those in which, with

her eyes turned heavenward, she says to the Father, 'Look at what you have done to me!' It isn't that I compare myself to Christ crucified, but simply that I often turn to the text of the Gospels to understand my situation. As Jack said, that book contains all the other books.

But doesn't the Virgin, that perfect being, say to the Father, 'Look at what they have done to him!', thereby acquitting the Father and the Son, assigning the guilty verdict to men, to those men who splashed my eyes with acid?

After deliberating with my inner jury, I find myself guilty in some ways, since everything began on a certain day in the 1830s, in the little port of Ouidah, on the Slave Coast, thanks to the complicity of the Sacha de Sousa, a trafficker in ebony flesh, and King Gezo, thanks to the complicity of the English, the Portuguese, the French, thanks to the complicity of all mankind, including myself. Say that on one or another of those boats, that year or some other year, there happened to be in that stinking, sick, terrified cargo two men sufficiently robust to survive the journey and also to survive the desperation that gave to some enough force to commit suicide by swallowing their own tongues. From the seeds of these two men sold at auction emerged the Harlem ghetto. And how can I explain, without seeming to be out of my mind, that these monsters from the ghetto are part of myself? Those two men are the very ones who came and attacked me.

A French television crew has come to ask me for an interview. My first impulse is to refuse, since an article in a women's magazine had displayed me like someone in a Grand Guignol scene, dripping with blood. I finally accept because it's the best way to reach out to my mother. I ask them to come film a day at the Lighthouse.

It's the first time I am confronted with the camera from the other side.

Instinctively, I take part in setting things up, deciding where to film, visualising through the camera's eye the message I want to convey. I get so interested in technical details, particularly the general lighting and the position of the spots, that when it is finally time for me to express myself, I'm almost too drained to be able to. I am afraid that all my mother will perceive is my exhaustion.

Later on, taxi drivers, passers-by, and other strangers mention having seen me. My mother seems to have been the only one who didn't watch television that evening.

FOURTEEN

The world has become, like God, invisible, and yet it is real. And God? The soul always moves from shadow towards light. Only desperate creatures hide in darkness, like sick animals. The hardest thing, in this dark labyrinth I am imprisoned in, is to go on believing in light. To re-create it and make it become a sort of halo within, I have to concentrate all my strength on this battle with shadow. In this quest, I follow a corridor plunging into darkness, which is like a crack within myself. Deep within me is the stench of stagnant waters in which the current of my life has been lost. My cry breaks the labyrinth's fractured maze and the song of the birds seems to be buried beneath Mount Everest. In this solitary struggle, neither Pascal's diversions nor Nietzsche's heroism can be of any help. And the mystic night is absolute, only slightly disturbed by the sulphuric presence of the Minotaur in the heart of darkness.

This morning I call death and I am ashamed, because I do not desire it out of fulfilment, but to disappear. And I am not even sure that death is a disappearance. Suicide? No. Orders are to go on living, meanly, painfully, scrupulously. Every day I work at my solitude, but all I am aware of is the absence of my life. I have been interned within myself, internal imprisonment, submitted to the temptation of the invisible. And morning after morning, the sun rises and the radio announces, 'Today, clear visibility.' Every morning they lie to me.

And then there was Valushka. She who came one evening to sit beside me, she who was the sister of the mythical Ariadne. But she had no need of the famous thread, because she was a bearer of light. She was lucifer. And by the sheer force of that light she pierced the dark labyrinth and reached me. Just when suffering was filling my insomnia with the tales of a thousand and one nights; just when I was refusing to consider that suffering – because the wound means nothing, only the dead eyes count; just when I was axing at myself with alcohol; just when I was tempted by the void announced by the darkness into which I have been thrown, just then, on a sofa, one night she came to sit beside me.

'I've just come back from the Island. I know you lived there a long time, and I'd like to talk to you about it.'

Her voice opens the darkness like the piercingly sweet sound of a flute at night.

She took me by surprise. I see the Island, the whole Island, the volcanoes, the rice paddies. Suddenly I am very far away, stunned by the splendid stillness, the meeting of water, earth, and sun, and the night defeated by the volcanoes. Up in the hills, the obsessive rhythm of gamelans almost drowns out the melancholy sound of bamboo flutes. The dazzling sea splashes me with unexpected spray. Outside, on the streets of New York, I hear the shrieking of police sirens, deep within the black labyrinth, the roaring of the Minotaur. How dare she speak to me of this self – of this vanished self, of myself drunk with wonder at the sight of this paradise reflected in the sea, drunk with solitude and yet open to every particle of the world?

'Don't talk to me about the Island. Please don't talk about it.'

If I am to remain imprisoned in the dark labyrinth, I must remember what the world is like. But the Island is something else. I must forget it. The Minotaur's horns are ripping into my stomach. To escape the temptation of suffering such evocations, I have retreated even farther into the labyrinth, where the darkness is more impenetrable, where no one can join me – above all, not that voice which is so feminine. So feminine that already I miss it, so filled with poetry that already I am wounded.

And slowly, in spite of everything, the Island emerges from the past, from another life. Women in multicoloured sarongs catch dragonflies, slowly waving long strips of gauze in transparent rice paddies. This child I met on top of the Batu Api mountain standing before a temple, gazing far beyond the horizon. The Island, an inverted reflection of paradise in the sea, is reversed again in the eyes of children.

There on the sofa I am swept along by those nights when thunder, music, volcano rumbles shake the Island. Nights when fearful battles take place between spirits and forces, when human beings shelter like ants and muster their courage by humming epic tales from the *Ramayana*. In the courtyard of the palace of Gianyar, three young girls, circled by torchlight, dance to the rhythm of music asleep with its gentleness, filling the night with golden reflections. And from a beach we watch night's retreat in its glorious explosion of mauve, purple, violet, and vermilion, revealing beyond the sea a brief glimpse of the immense, fabled, mythical volcano of Lombok.

All it took was for that voice to say to me, 'I've just come back from the Island.' How dare she?

'Don't talk about the Island!'

I would have liked to say it to her gently, but my voice sounds rough.

There is a silence and a sudden absence. She has gone.

Around me there is a confusion of conversations.

I ask Claire, who has brought me a glass of wine:

'Who was here a minute ago?'

'Valushka.'

'Where is she?'

'Here.'

'I know, but where?'

Claire says, lowering her voice:

'Right there, next to you, sitting on the rug.'

My heart turns numb. I lean towards Claire and whisper:

'What is she doing?'

'She is looking at you.'

And I hear, 'She loves you.'

I put out my hand and my fingers touch a cloud of hair that I already know to be blonde. In the midst of these people, your stillness reaches out towards me. I look at you, and through my steel glasses I feel your piercing glances. I see your long, dark, sad eyes. Forced within myself, my sight sees through my whole

body; my lips are two eyelids. All my energy looks at you. The
groaning of the Minotaur is inaudible. The darkness is already
in retreat. The walls of the labyrinth are cracking. Very softly,
I ask:

'You are there?'

'Yes.'

And in her voice, I hear all the evidence of her acceptance.

And I hear 'I love you.' And I hear 'This love is forbidden.'

The air becomes rarefied around us, and we inhale it together.
A magic circle surrounds us, which no one dares to cross. No
one follows her across the boundaries of the labyrinth, which
she tremulously enters.

We remain still, riveted by this absent gaze. My body is worn
out by the struggle in which I both attract and repel her. If she
enters any farther, she will scream with fear. I break the circle,
get up and leave. In certain cases, it is easier to be inhuman,
and alone. Perhaps she is not aware of how much her gaze
makes me suffer. No, it is not her gaze; it is her love. When
she answered 'Yes,' she offered herself completely, and to be
united with her heart, mine has been wrenched from my side.
You were wearing, that evening, the delicate scent of tuberose.

I leave with this wound, refusing to recognise it. I leave,
confidently believing in the absurd, proud illusion that I am the
master of my life, free to forbid love. A love forbidden anyway,
for you are not free, Valushka.

FIFTEEN

Autumn, a melancholy season on the East Coast, suddenly reveals its presence by setting the maple trees on fire. En route to Claire's house in the country, I breathe a stagnant smell beneath the leaves. Now I am living in a seedy apartment on First Avenue. Every morning I must dust from my face a fine powder of plaster that has fallen from the ceiling during the night. The bathtub is in the kitchen. During the day a zinc cover transforms it into a table. It is a sad place, which smells of poor emigrants of the beginning of the century. The interior decoration is the achievement of a homosexual hairdresser. Mirrors and little plastic cherubs. 'A Moroccan brothel,' says Jallen, a friend of mine who was born in Tangier.

Désirée wore herself out trying to clean it up, but to no avail. The filth of the whole city has formed a crust in this railroad flat. My fingers meet sticky surfaces. Everything is filthy. The rooms are laid out in a row. The living room with its two windows on the avenue, shaken by trucks. No window in the bedroom. No window in the bar. No window in the dining room. The kitchen-bathroom at last has a window. The place is a test tube for growing bacteria.

Nonetheless, I must gain time. To escape these dreary surroundings, I go out as often as I can with Jallen. One afternoon we go for a walk in Central Park. Returning, we wait for the bus. When I at last hear the pneumatic sigh of the doors as they open, I throw away my cigarette and get in. As I sit down, I hear Jallen giggling beside me.

'What's so funny?'

'Nothing much. Except that you tossed your cigarette into

the handbag of a woman who was getting off, and now she's walking along with a big trail of smoke behind her.'

'Doesn't she realise it?'

'No. The wind is against her.'

The process of rehabilitation, which began scarcely two months ago, is slow. In spite of an excellent 'facial vision', as they call it, which helps me detect obstacles, I'm still practising on the fifth-floor corridor of the Lighthouse. Lesley, the instructor I've been assigned to, teaches me how to make even arcs with my cane. I advance my right foot, the cane touches the floor to my left. I advance my left foot, the cane traces an arc and touches the floor to my right. Whether or not I progress in a straight line depends on how uniform the arc is. The monotony of this exercise is not relieved by any sense of humour. At the end of one session, having forgotten my tape recorder on Lesley's desk, I retrace my steps in a hurry with my open hand held out in front of me so that I can locate the edge of the desk. A female instructor is leaning over the desk and whispering something to Lesley. Carried along by my momentum, I find myself with my hand on her ass. Instead of quickly withdrawing it and apologising, I feel around, and announce, 'This is not my tape recorder,' as I leave the room in deadly silence.

And so every day, for two hours, I practise in the same corridor, which leads to the Music Department. I hear pianos, flutes, and, above all, appalling operatic singing. The blind are very musical, but not all of them.

I am also learning how to use the staircases without danger. Actually, I have been taking the elevator as seldom as possible ever since the day a blind fellow grabbed hold of me and threw me out because I was in the way when he wanted to get off.

The strange laughter, the cynicism, and the smells would have been enough to turn me off. Day follows day, monotonously. I also avoid the cafeteria, preferring to fast in one of the Music Department's soundproof studios. I practise my scales and experiment with simple improvisations. I have no musical memory except for a gamelan piece I heard night after night in the villages of the Island five years ago. That's the only thing I know how to play, so I play it over and over ad nauseam. Once a week, the teacher shows me how to play easy little pieces that bore me – they all sound too much like 'Twinkle, twinkle, little star.'

I sometimes spend three hours in that airless room. I go away somewhat dizzy but soothed. Piano is my Valium; it is also my diet, and that does me no harm, because I am feeling uncomfortable with my body, which is getting heavier and stockier. My body does not flow anymore.

My Braille music teacher, a blind woman whose husband is also blind, has a habit of always saying 'we' and 'they' which by itself is enough to annoy me. She tries to draw me into the world of the blind. She is also completely devoid of a sense of humour. In short, she is very blind.

She uses her harsh, high-pitched voice not only to communicate but also to guide herself by bouncing it off the walls, like radar. Her dog, so disciplined with its harness on, becomes playful when the harness is taken off and will come over to lick one's hands. When he is wearing the harness, I hear him dreaming and groaning under the piano.

With one hand I am supposed to follow the music and with the other play the corresponding note on the piano. I point out to her:

'All that is fine, but when you have to play a piece with both hands, it really isn't practical. Do you think that, with a certain amount of practice, it would be possible to sit on a Braille score and read it that way, using both hands to play?'

She is indignant, goes off to register a complaint with the head of the Music Department, and refuses to continue my lessons!

During these months of rehabilitation, I spent several hundred hours at the piano, on a sort of leave of absence from myself and from life.

I like the smell of the piano and physical contact with it. No other instrument appeals to me, but then, I am completely ignorant when it comes to music. I buy recordings of Chopin's twenty-four Etudes by Samson François and Madame Davidoff, and I compare them. My ear becomes educated and the word *interpretation* acquires a new meaning.

I attend concerts, including some by hysterical pianists like Cecil Taylor. I go to the Village Gate and especially to West Boondock Bar, where the drinkers are often more professional than the regular pianist. There are only blacks except for a Dutch waitress from Amsterdam.

Henry the barman, whom I have known for three years, shakes my hand when he sees me again for the first time and states decisively:

'It doesn't matter.'

Well, since he says so! He offers me a glass of 055 rum, which for some unknown reason we call Water Proof. Two glasses and you forget your address.

I recognise the atmosphere on my skin. Tonight there is an excellent double-bass player being massacred by the pianist. The bar is packed. Jallen, who has come with me, feels uncomfortable. I slip my hand under her arm and gently press her hand, which she has put in her pocket. I stroke it to reassure her. Just then I hear her voice on the other side of me:

'Stop holding hands with that guy!'

We head for home. We are at 17th Street, near the docks on the Hudson, and the area is deserted. It's getting late. We need to find a taxi. It's so cold that even the muggers must be at home. I can sense how relieved Jallen is when a taxi on 14th Street slides up to us through the snow.

'You're crazy! Why do you go to places like that after what they did to you?'

'Who do you mean?'

'Blacks.'

'It's not the blacks.'

I keep running up against that generalisation over and over again. Nothing can be done about it: Harlem, Voodoo, crime, blacks – it is all linked forever in their heads.

It was about this time that I found Bandigo again. Bandigo is a bay horse I had ridden ten years ago in the forest of Shelter

Island. By coincidence, through various sales, he had ended up in this part of New York State.

I remember him very clearly as being impulsive but not tricky and decide to ride him again. A man warns me:

'He's a nasty one. Two months ago he threw me against a tree and broke my leg.'

I ask to be left alone in his stall and speak to him very gently, blowing softly into his nostrils so that he can breathe my smell and get to know me. I look him straight in the eyes, hoping he will understand the absence of my sight.

Outside, I jump into the saddle and it is as if it had been yesterday. But as soon as he moves and begins to dance in the brisk cold air, I get vertigo, I have completely lost touch with the ground, I float in space.

Under me this animal brings back a longing for freedom, for gallops, for large open spaces, for everything that I am now denied.

The walls of my prison will not dissolve.

With relief I move from the dusty railroad flat to an apartment on Park Avenue. My lease includes Ernestine and the cat.

Ernestine is a tiny seventy-five-year-old woman from Brittany. While doing the housework she talks to me about a certain Monsieur Marcel.

'Oh, la-la, Monsieur Marcel! As soon as he saw me, he'd whistle.'

One day with a sorry voice she tells me:

'When you're born stupid, you remain stupid all your life! This morning I read in the paper that some of Monsieur Marcel's drawings were sold for thousands of dollars. Well now, he gave me some, yes, he did, and just think, I don't know where I put them. It seems to me I may have used them to wrap up some shoes. When you're born stupid . . .'

I ask for more details:

'What was Monsieur Marcel's name?'

She answers, as if it were obvious:

'Why, Monsieur Marcel Duchamp. He was a friend of Monsieur Scott Fitzgerald, I worked for him for many years.

I'm the one who raised their daughter, Mademoiselle Scottie. So I really knew Monsieur Duchamp! He wasn't like Monsieur Hemingway – what a real rough one he was! But the nicest of all was Monsieur Dos Passos.'

The cat has no tales to tell. He is even odiously silent. He has got into the habit of falling asleep in the armchair at the desk where I work. And when I try to sit down, I am attacked by such a storm of clawing and spitting that I jump up with my heart in my mouth. A cat is probably the only animal that can become completely unreal in an apartment for someone who doesn't see. He moves about noiselessly and settles down in unlikely spots. This one jumps from the floor to the back of a chair, then onto a shelf over my bed and stays there, watching me. When I stretch out my hand for a cassette to listen to some music or a recorded book, my fingers plunge into this warm, furry thing. The cat was a problem. And then, little by little, I noticed that I could hear him and follow his movements. My ear had become sharper, I had learned how to listen to the cat, who had nothing to say.

In this apartment my insomnia wakes me up very early in the morning. The rhythm of the trains rumbling underground tells me the time. This digestion starts around five-thirty, accelerates until eight, and then slows down. Metropolitan monster, cannibalistic megalopolis, a flood of slaves flows under Park Avenue. I hear the sound of this swallowing and digesting before the defecation at Grand Central Station. And yet we all want to be tributaries of the tribe. Even to the point of being part of the enslavement. My bed is a still bank alongside the flowing river.

Someone mentions the resignation that can be found in the works of Vargas, the Peruvian writer. And I say there is no resignation because someone who writes five hundred pages on resignation proclaims his own revolt. It is, in fact, the role of the artist to fight against submission. This huge suburban area around New York is full of resignation. Let doubt live within us, but not abdication.

With Vargas one feels the anger, the indignation, and the frustration. And all that leads to creativity, the opposite of resignation.

One feels the passionate look he aims at others, at life. The last sentence of his book, 'We will all die,' is not even pessimistic, for freedom is the knowledge of death.

SIXTEEN

Helped by a most beautiful Indian summer, I prepare myself. Three days of swimming and sun on top of an 85th Street skyscraper and I will arrive in Paris with a tan, in great shape, armed to ward off any pity. I don't want to be mistaken for a victim.

At Kennedy, I discover that being blind makes it easier to travel than to stay at home. One of the airline's employees takes me in hand. I hang onto his arm as if I were hooked up to a factory assembly line. I become a product being processed. Stamped, frisked, weighed; it's all done mechanically. Automatically a young woman at the counter asks me:

'Would you like a window seat?'

I answer with a straight face:

'We fly so high these days that you can't see very much.'

Almost seven hours later, Charles de Gaulle Airport. The employees there have prepared a wheelchair, which I absolutely refuse to use. They insist, assuring me that in cases like mine it is customary. But nothing will get me to sit in that chair; I'd rather crawl down the corridors. I am blind, not paralysed, a difficult customer.

They send for a hostess, a Martinican. I hold onto her arm, again as if on an assembly line. On our way to customs, I bump my head against a television set that was placed too low.

'Watch where you're going!' she says, reproachfully.

It amazes me to hear so many people speaking French and to realise that the smell of Gauloise cigarettes is everywhere, even on my father, who marks this special occasion by embracing me.

*   *   *

The simple sound of the key turning in the lock is familiar, like my father's limp, a war wound.

'After you.'

I enter with the confidence that comes from knowing the place so well and bump right into my mother's soft body, especially so now from lack of exercise. She stands there silently, leaning on her canes. Gently, I kiss her.

'You must make some sort of sound, or I'm afraid I'll knock you over.'

She stammers. I become impatient, since, as I have said, I don't want to be a cause of pain or pity to my mother. She who, in spite of a Japanese-sounding name, Yo, is the epitome of the Irish mother. She to whom I would pour out my anecdotes, adventures, and souvenirs from trips to Asia, the Americas, or Africa, like a sailor throwing open his trunk before the dazzled eyes of his sweetheart. I want no one's pity, least of all hers. I slip away from her embrace and try to pass between her and the hall table. My aluminium cane taps against her. And that's where old Irish blood helps. The black humour of the situation becomes instantaneously apparent, and she bursts out laughing. She leans on my shoulder on the way to the living room, a way so familiar I could run down it.

Later, when the three of us go out into the street, my mother with her two crutches, my father with his bamboo cane, and I with my antenna, she says:

'We look like a centipede going out for a walk.'

I'm curious to observe the way people react, without judging them, but, rather, discovering what lies ahead and what I will have to fight against. Friends who have disappeared for years begin to show up again, alerted by some kind of tom-tom. Hubert was at the Naval Academy, and is an officer. Our paths had not crossed since then. He comes to see me. When he rings the bell, I open the door myself.

'Hi!'

No answer, but a strange sound. I have the distinct impression that . . . I bend down slowly with my hand stretched out in front of me and find him in a dead faint on the doormat. He gets up right away, insists that it's nothing, just a slight indisposition, and then falls down again. The situation is rather embarrassing, and when he's feeling better, I confess to him that I don't have quite the same confidence I had before in our country's great Navy.

It is difficult for my mother and me to communicate. We try, but I am afraid of her emotions and she is afraid of my toughness.

'Wouldn't it be better to wear regular glasses? That steel is a bit cruel.'

'I know.'

And still our love is so strong that we try to reestablish the complicity formed in my house on Capri. Already half paralysed with arthritis, she had to be brought up from the port in a wicker chair perched on the back of a truck normally used to deliver tanks of Butagaz for cooking and heating. It was winter, there were no tourists, and the people of Capri can deal with such things. In that sea gulls' nest high above the Faraglioni and the sea, we had grown to know each other, not without turmoil. 'I don't need a mother anymore' was false and true, but it had to be said in order to break the established taboos. I had to build up another mother, one I could choose. Several times she said, 'How do you dare speak to me that way?' But it was the only way to speak the truth.

Little by little, the situation with my family becomes more defused and I find my place again. In the living room my father is standing on a ladder and, with the help of my younger brother, Thibault, is hanging a painting of Saint Peter. The frame is heavy and the job isn't easy. When the portrait is finally hung, I point out:

'It seems a little low to me.'

My father, from the top of the ladder, defends his point of view:

'Do you think so? It looks all right to me.'

For several seconds I delight in pursuing this absurd conversation, until my father catches on.

Thibault reads me adventure stories, which we both enjoy

immensely. One evening we run across the true story of the captain of a felucca sailing off the coast of Yemen. Some sort of disease was causing him gradually to lose his sight. He was one of the best captains on the Red Sea and navigation was his whole life. Fearing that the crew might notice his blindness, he had his eldest son come aboard and, pretending to be teaching him the art of navigation, said to him, 'Son, describe the coast as we go along.' For a time, through his son's eyes, he was able to prolong his life as a sailor.

I make it clear that, from now on, I fully intend to go on living my life, that I am neither desperate nor broken, nor am I a better person, unfortunately. I have not changed, the grace of the Lord has not touched me. Almost ten years have passed since I last lived in France. I feel a certain anxiety; everyone defends his ideas, his values, like a dog clings to its bone, even though there's no meat left on it. I find myself in the position of an African whose idols are going to be overturned by some white Father. In all that, there is a lack of respect. The other day, on the radio, I was pleased to hear the Pope, turning his attention to China, apologise for the disrespectful conduct of certain missionaries in past centuries. Certain martyrdoms were pure justice. As Aho says, 'We have been too trusting and they ruined everything.'

The situation is hardly helped when a girlfriend comes by to pick me up one evening. Tightly curled hair, cruel red lipstick, long legs in skintight black leather, high heels. Abomination of abominations! The sin! I sense my family's consternation. I don't see what spiritual evolution has to do with emasculation. In fact, this young woman helps me keep in touch with current events. The misunderstanding can be enormous, and I will not be believed, since my life has hardly been one of a saint; there are precedents that hardly speak well for me. I just go on repeating, provocatively:

'I have received and I have given a great deal through the sins of the flesh.'

To which is answered:

'Woe to the man from whom the offence cometh.'

SEVENTEEN

'No, really, I don't think so, I'm too tired.'

I came back from Paris two days ago and have just moved again. In eight months I have moved seven times, and that has had a positive effect on my rehabilitation. There are two choices: either to be immobilised by organisation or to move on in spite of disorganisation.

On the telephone, Claire's voice insists, but tonight I don't want to see anyone.

'Bach on the guitar! For two hours, it may be a bit long.'

She insists.

'You can't do this to me. I promised Valushka that you'd be there.'

'What does Valushka want? I don't understand. She . . .'

'Don't be silly! It's not at all what you think. She just wants to talk with you.'

'In that case I'll come.'

The guitarist is uninspired and under his fingers Bach sounds repetitious. You are seated beside me, listening in silence. You have not said a word, but in the lobby I greeted you by holding your long, slender fingers in mine. And then you took my arm so that I could lead you to our seats. With anyone else, it would have been a mistake. But miraculously, silently, we reached our seats.

Despite the monotony of the music, you seem to be listening attentively. I feel nothing, neither you nor the music. What you said to me with your silence two months ago must have been dreamt. And then all of a sudden I feel your breath on me.

'Let's go.'

My heart comes to a stop.

'Sorry?'

'Do you really want to hear the whole concert?'

'Not really.'

'Then let's leave. I've fixed some supper, if you would like it.'

I agree and we go off, leaving the others slightly amazed. We go to her apartment.

Laid out on a table is a cold light supper. How could she be sure I'd come? This idea disturbs me. I put up my own defence, and remain on the surface of myself, impervious.

'I wanted you to come here so you could listen to something.'

She gets up. A few seconds later her footsteps return and near my head I hear a strange gurgle.

'What is it?' she asks.

'Water.'

'What water?'

'I don't know,' I say, laughing.

'You should know.'

She brings the object close to my ear and I hear the ocean.

'It's a shell, a shell that has imprisoned the sea.'

'Which sea?'

And that is how she broke down my defences, for at the same time she burned incense and sandalwood from the Island. The conch in my hand echoes the Java Sea. I feel like crying because she is so beautiful and she dares to bring me the Island. When she comes near, I feel her skirt brush up against me, and I am overwhelmed by desire. All I can do is keep telling myself, 'Don't touch her, don't touch her.' She is for me a forbidden city. My hand must not approach her light. And immediately my fingers come to rest gently on her cotton skirt, on her thigh. For some absurd reason, I am reminded of a scene from an old movie in which a pirate sets fire to a keg of powder by puffing his pipe on it and blows everything up. We, too, explode. The damp, dark labyrinth explodes. Ignored, the Minotaur writhes in agony. She is my incestuous sister, and we tremble with the joy of our reunion.

I have already lost my head in the ethereal cloud of gold that is your hair and with a sigh, you say:

'Not here.'

And every night you return to my apartment, where there is nothing but a narrow mattress on the wooden floor, a piano, a red telephone, and later on a tree you give me.

You have the spontaneous grace and elegance of ancient races. I see you arched by desire like a rainbow. A thousand colours shimmer beneath my skin, and I long to breathe the golden light surrounding you. The underside of your arms, when you stretch them out towards me, has the softness of a bat's wing and your breath is the sigh of an inner garden. I love you, I love all of you, I love everything that is you. In this dance, never was a flower more open; lids are pierced by a Cyclopean eye. In the act of love, she makes me see. Only her sleeping presence by my side can obliterate the horror of blackness. All that beauty lying there, in the cloud of her blonde hair. Her breath which I breathe, leaning over to join her in the distant world of her sleep. Her scent, her warmth, the weight of her body, all this love. Just now she said, 'Close your eyes, sleep,' and I felt a bit strange, thinking of my sealed eyelids. If I open my eyes, she is going to disappear, so it's better that my eyelids are sewn together. When Valushka kisses my eyelids, my belly is ripped apart. I would like to be engulfed in love, push aside all fear, any trace of suspicion.

EIGHTEEN

People stop me on Madison Avenue and ask if I'm involved in an experiment or if I'm practising to be an instructor for the blind. They don't want to recognise the fact that I am blind.

The American method of rehabilitation is so effective that it gives rise to misunderstandings.

I take such big strides that it was hard for the people at the Lighthouse to find a cane long enough. This cane, made of fibreglass, vibrates between my fingers like a violin string. It transmits such precise information that I am able to move along very quickly. Shopkeepers call out, 'Are you crazy? Slow down. You're going to kill somebody.' They are absolutely right. In fact, I have already thrown several people to the ground. The technique, which is quite accidental, consists of thrusting the tip of my cane between the ankles of whoever is walking in front of me. This is particularly effective with women teetering along in high heels. I hear them go down clinging to their handbags, the contents of which clatter onto the sidewalk. Bystanders start to shout but are often drowned out by the insults of an indignant husband. This technique sometimes has an unexpected effect on the puritanical ladies of Park Avenue. One woman between whose legs I had inserted my cane turned around furiously to protest. Pablo, an Italian friend who was with me, answered with great dignity:

'Well, madam, better that than nothing.'

Another time, getting off the bus, I felt a slight brushing against the cane as I pointed it down towards the sidewalk. It was so slight that I paid no attention to it. At that moment, I heard the soft voice of a little old woman coming from the gutter under the bus:

'Bravo, young man, you practically killed me.'

Just then a woman ran up, shouting:

'I saw it all! I saw it all! It's not his fault. He didn't do anything.'

'Madam, that's not the point. Let's just make sure the bus doesn't start up and run over her.'

Mario, a Cuban friend I had lost track of for seven years, is in New York for a while. He was sitting in a bar and, in the way such things so often happen in this city, he struck up a conversation with a man sitting next to him. After a minute or two, Mario said to him:

'It's strange, but you have the same smile as one of my friends. In fact, he was living in New York.' And he told him about what had happened to me. The man answered:

'But he's still living in New York! I can even tell you where. Besides, he's not as blind as he pretends.'

It so happens that he is the boyfriend of the girl who lives just above me, and every day he sees me racing down the stairs of our little building.

That's how one morning Mario showed up at my door. Like all the members of his family, Cubans in exile, Mario is a remarkable pianist. He seats himself at the Steinway, strikes some chords, launches into Rachmaninoff. I am not that surprised to see him, since he comes from a family of which you can expect anything. In Cuba, his grandmother had challenged Hemingway to a boxing match. The writer, greatly amused, was prancing about in front of the old lady when she came at him with a tremendous uppercut. At that time, these fabulously wealthy planters lived in a newly built medieval castle in the midst of fields of sugar cane. They had imported albino elephants from Asia, and the young daughters were enchanted by the pinkness of their hide. But this power, this extravagance had been acquired only at the expense of much blood. Once, in the course of suppressing a slave revolt, the head of the family had had their grand carriage brought out; in it he placed his wife and children dressed in velvet and lace; and on the two lead horses he stretched out the black, bloody bodies of the two leaders of the revolt. This strange cortege paraded around the plantation while the slaves looked on in terror.

The family arrived years later in France, exiled by Fidel Castro, but still at the height of their power. They were so rich that the minister of finance requested that they keep him informed of their investments. So much spilling of blood doomed the family two generations later. First there was the dramatic leap of the eldest daughter from the top of the Arc de Triomphe. Then, a gold mine in southwestern France swallowed up billions of francs and never produced a single nugget. Three hundred workers dug for ten years. All this defies explanation unless one takes into account the amount of pride involved. Such are my reflections as I listen to the all-too-sensitive playing of this young man whom destiny has brought to my doorstep.

One evening, a week later, the melodies seem to spiral downward, becoming sadder and stranger. I call out:

'Mario!'

No answer. I keep on calling, but he remains obstinately silent. And soon the playing stops. I am filled with apprehension.

'Mario!'

I can't even hear him breathe. Fear begins to grip me. Suicide, destruction, madness, blood. What if he were to go to the kitchen without my hearing him, take a knife, and destroy us both?

'Mario?'

With my hands outstretched, I slowly approach the piano stool. He is slumped forward with his head on the piano keys. I touch his shoulder, and he begins to sob quietly, as do people whose sorrows began long ago. I shake him gently, and he falls to the floor. Not a word, no reaction of any kind. I understand that something is seriously wrong. He must be taken to the hospital at once. I get him into his coat and walk him down to the street. His movements are spasmodic and he walks like a malfunctioning robot.

At the corner of Madison and 63rd Street, I say to him:

'When you see a taxi, let me know and I'll flag it down.'

The cold air seems to revive him, for he answers:

'OK.'

I hardly recognise his voice. It's about 1:00 A.M. and I am frozen. I'm getting worried.

'You haven't seen a taxi?'

'Yes, I have,' his dull voice answers.

'I told you to let me know. Do you understand? When you see a taxi, say so.'

We wait for at least another ten minutes and this time, without much hope, I ask him:

'No taxi?'

'Yes. There have been some.'

Exasperated, I let go of him and station myself in the middle of Madison Avenue with my arm up. In three minutes a taxi pulls up.

'Lenox Hill Hospital!'

We go about a dozen blocks.

At the hospital, the doctors on duty tell me:

'He's a manic depressive going through a severe crisis. We've got to give him shock treatment.'

Mario is still not showing any more reaction than a vegetable. As far as I am concerned, shock treatment is out of the question.

Mount Sinai Hospital is not far away. I seize him by the arm. The street is deserted, but which of us is in any kind of condition to guide the other, the mad one or the blind one? I try to make use of whatever wits Mario still has about him.

'Walk straight ahead to the next intersection.'

We walk along and suddenly the sky is no longer above us. Our steps resound, obviously, we are in some kind of lobby.

'Where are we, in a building?'

'Yes.'

'Do you have something to do here?'

'No.'

What has happened is that he has done nothing to correct my old tendency to veer to the left, trailing along beside me as if under strict orders.

Once we are back on the street, I stop relying on him. Obviously I must take the lead. With him in tow, I reach the Psychiatric Ward at Mount Sinai. The doctors on duty ask Mario what my problem is. I have the strange feeling, behind my steel glasses, that the orderlies are going to come after me with a strait jacket, especially since Mario isn't saying a word.

The next three hours are cheerfully spent trying to get Mario to sign his admission form. In exasperation, the doctor tells me:

'It's your problem.'

I protest:

'No, it isn't!'

He goes out of the room and leaves me alone with Mario, whom I try to reason with.

At 4:00 A.M., when another shift takes over, an older, more dogmatic doctor arrives. Thanks to Dr Freud, he has immediately diagnosed his patient – at least, he thinks he has.

'Look, my friend, it won't do you any good to close yourself off. I'm here to help you. I am not your father.'

I hear a scornful snort from Mario and the rustle of the admission form as he signs it.

Lying in bed, Mario groans:

'I'm doomed, doomed. . . .'

The monologue that follows is disjointed. Suddenly I have the impression that his voice is getting lower and lower. I have a doubt and ask:

'Mario, where are you?'

'Under the bed.'

'What are you doing there?'

'I don't know. It feels good here, I feel protected.'

'Well, if it feels good, OK, go ahead and stay there.'

And I, too, sit down on the floor, to be at the same level. Naturally, it is at this moment that the door opens. I hear the Freudian doctor shout:

'For heaven's sake, what's going on in here?'

Once again I imagine them coming at me with a strait jacket.

NINETEEN

Violent by nature, I have had to learn to be gentle. Gentle when I trip on the curb, gentle when I run into things, gentle when I bump my head. I have had to learn patience. But what has become of this violence? It must be there, lurking somewhere, intact, unquenched, and frustrated. I now touch women with gentleness instead of taking them with violence. Since I cannot see and be appeased by her beauty, there is no longer any place in me for brutality. Only touching her body can reintroduce beauty to me. I want to feel her skin, caress her, be caressed, that being the next closest thing to seeing. It's like having an eye at the end of my penis.

Some evenings, defeated with fatigue and alcohol, with my reeducation and a creeping existence, I fall asleep fully clothed, sometimes on the rug, without even touching the dinner so carefully prepared by Désirée. For a period these crises occurred two or three times a month. They ended that day in May when I was sitting on a wooden bench in a corridor at the Lighthouse. The air was suddenly filled with the scent I had recently come to know. I sense her presence but am not sure. My whole being is on the alert, listening. A thick piece of paper with writing in Braille on it is placed in my hand. My fingertips read:

'I love you.'

Convulsive beauty will either be erotic, veiled, explosive, unchanging, magical, circumstantial – or it will not be.

'André Breton: "L'Amour fou."'

She has crouched down; I feel her breath on my fingers and I take her head in my hands. Cascades of hair flow from beneath a little Japanese cap, which comes down over her ears. She is trembling. She has entered the tomb, this wintry labyrinth, and taking me by the hand, without a word, she leads me back towards life, allowing me to guide her.

I lead her to the seashore, at the far end of Long Island. For the first time, I hear the sound of the ocean without seeing it, and I am overwhelmed by my hate of all those long days and nights of solitude and darkness. It is enough for her hand to touch mine, her voice to murmur in my ear, and I am overwhelmed by light. What has happened to that weariness that struck me down into bed, comatose, long before sundown? That feeling of failure at the end of a day has vanished. I am cleansed, resuscitated by love, and there is this strength, which I thought I had lost forever.

With her fingernail, she slowly traces the seam of my joined eyelids. I sense that she wishes her nail were a blade to open them up and restore my sight. The ocean shivers along the shore. The cry of a sea gull leaves a sad note of distress, which, although unspoken, sits silently between us. On this first day of spring, there is something pure about the song of the earth. Before us, the meditative, vast Atlantic. And on the warm sand your love like a cool spring. All this frees my heart, which murmurs these words, so simple, so dangerous: 'I love you.' So dangerous, for in saying it I hand you the knife which opens me up entirely.

Beneath my fingers your body transforms and blooms. Your voice, too, is lower, slower, more melodious; your movements more enchanting. There is a secret. You are Russian. A dancer with Balanchine destined for the stars. You left it all behind. There is a secret that perhaps you are not aware of. One day when you were with me going to a shabby suite in the old, once-elegant Ansonia Hotel where I rented a piano for several hours a week, we went by a building on 68th Street, the Dorchester. You asked me to go into the lobby with you, and there you started to cry.

'This is where I used to live when I was sixteen and dancing in Monsieur Balanchine's company. I was lonely. Sixteen and alone in New York, with a strict governess and the company. All that was expected of us was to have perfect, anonymous bodies, faces didn't count. Monsieur Balanchine didn't like faces, and we vomited to remain thin.'

But that isn't what you are crying about. It's having betrayed your life of dance, music, sheer poetry; it's having turned your back on the performances, the audiences, the seedy dressing rooms from which you would emerge in radiant splendour. What you are crying over is the betrayed child. Later on, you let me explore the inner depths of that childhood.

I love you, Valushka, and I am frightened because you are poetry itself and I cannot show you the beauty of the world. And it is this suffering that is echoed by the sea gulls. With your Slavic sensitivity, you caught the scent of the Minotaur and I felt you shudder.

'How can you accept to remain like that?'

With this question you destroyed the golden peace of that late afternoon. This subject makes me feel uncomfortable, maybe I have accepted my fate too easily. The absence of revolt or collapse seems to me almost inhuman. Sometimes I wonder if this blindness did not weld the contradictions within my character, forcing harmony on me. As always I feel a certain distance from my life since we come from eternity and return to it. And here you are asking me to shorten that distance and to go and fight in the arena.

As I listen, I realise that what you really want to say is 'How can you accept the idea of defeat and organise your life around it? Stop being reasonable. Accept the thought, however crazy it is, that you might see again.'

And since, deep down, I am afraid of hope, I repeat, 'For the moment there is nothing to be done. That's what Dr T. keeps saying.' But your voice is shrill with indignation: 'Dr T.! It's not as if there were only Dr T.! I've never heard of Dr T.!' I am enchanted by this display of Slavic rationality, implying that it would be perfectly natural for you to know all the eye surgeons in the United States. Your logic has that unswerving quality I admire in the heroines of Russian novels.

One evening you tell me, reproachfully:

'You can't say "I love you" without taking me. Those are words followed by no action.'

This morning she showed up very early, a little out of breath, extremely exhilarated.

'There!' She presses a sheet of paper into my hands. 'It's a list of the eight best eye surgeons in the United States. One of them, Dr K., practises in New York. Phone him right away – here's his office number.'

She has caught me unprepared.

'It's eight-thirty; he won't be in his office yet.'

'Yes, he will! He works tremendously hard.'

But all I do is get his secretary, who won't put me through and offers me an appointment in two months. Valushka says:

'Phone back! Insist. You weren't clear enough. Maybe she thought you just wanted to have some glasses made! You really don't know how to get things done. You sounded like somebody who wanted to see him about a sty.'

And she goes off in a gust of wind from the Russian steppes, banging the door shut.

The next day, towards the end of the afternoon, the telephone rings, and in a lilting, triumphant voice, she announces:

'You have an appointment with Dr K. Thursday at nine.'

'But . . .' But she has already hung up. I call her back.

'Will you come with me?'

'Of course!'

Thursday, we are in Dr K.'s suite of offices. It's obvious that he is extremely important. Nurses coming and going, phones constantly ringing, Japanese-style interior decoration, with diplomas on the wall from the University of Tokyo.

Name, date of birth, and other uninteresting items are fed into a computer. But the secretary misspells my name three times and we have to start all over again. I lose patience and mutter in French, 'She is as thick as shit!' She finally gets the thing right and in perfect French invites us to go into the waiting room.

'So you speak French!'

'I am Canadian, monsieur,' she answers icily.

Valushka is nervous, hypersensitive. Whenever someone goes by, she squeezes my hand. Her anxiety is painful and makes me fear the verdict. I feel detached and want to remain so. Suddenly her hand tightens around mine.

'I've seen him. He has just gone by. Oh, Hugues! He looks just awful. He's ugly, with bulging eyes, like a big fat butcher, with no feelings. He's wearing a cowboy belt. Let's go, please, let's go right away. I have such a bad feeling about him!'

I recognise that Russian rationality of hers, which I don't understand at all but which at least has the advantage of continually surprising me.

'Go if you like, but I'm staying.'

'He looks so insensitive.'

Just then, the secretary calls out my name and we go into Dr K.'s consulting room. I sit down next to the desk. Without a word Valushka takes a seat somewhere behind me. Dr K. listens to me in silence, then asks me to place my head in an apparatus that I know only too well. I insert my face between the steel support for my forehead and the plastic chin rest. A light goes on and I feel the doctor's fingers gently trying to separate my eyelids. A shout coming from behind me makes us both jump.

'Don't touch his eyes!'

I take my head out of the apparatus and say, with a mixture of embarrassment and wonder:

'Valushka, if you are nervous, wait for me outside.'

She doesn't answer and the examination continues. Slowly, cautiously, the doctor's fingertips feel my shrivelled eyeballs through the thin skin. He notes that there is some perception of light, then turns off the machine. I sit up. The muscles in my back are in knots.

'If I were you or if you were my son,' he says in a calm, warm voice, 'I'd go see Dr A. in Barcelona. He has developed and perfected an operation called odonto-keratoprosthesis. It was invented by Dr Charleux, a Frenchman, and Dr Strampelli, an Italian. I'll explain it to you briefly. It involves inserting an artificial lens in the eye. First of all, they extract a tooth, generally a canine, and they cut off the bony part of the root.

The lens is placed into this cone, which is inserted in the cheek beneath the eye. It is left there for three months so that the root and the lens become covered by a thin organic film, which will lessen the chances of rejection. The whole thing is then implanted in the eye, and if it is successful, you obtain a kind of vision called tunnel vision. Naturally, since it is focused on infinity, you will be able to see a street number six blocks away very clearly but will have trouble reading a sign right in front of you. However, in some cases, the patient can even read a book. I have a film of this operation on video cassette right here. If you'd like, I'll show it to you, and your friend can describe what's happening.'

I don't feel much interest in Dr K.'s film if he isn't there himself to explain it, but I don't dare tell him so.

'Can you give me Dr A.'s address and tell me how to get in touch with him?'

The secretary brings in this information and I hear Dr K. writing.

For the second time, Valushka's voice pipes up:

'And write legibly, please!'

The pen stops and there is a moment of silence. Then, with feigned amiability, the great man replies:

'If you'd like, madam, come behind my chair and check while I write.'

Valushka has already stood up and moves over behind his shoulder. I can just imagine her attentive face, without the slightest trace of laughter, which I restrain in myself. Suddenly she speaks again:

'Is that an *e*?'

And she must be pointing her finger at what he has scribbled.

But the doctor has understood that what he has before him is a phenomenon of love, that this young woman of twenty-four has decided to fight for me, that she has no time for politeness or humour. For her, every second of my blindness is one second too many, and she doesn't want to leave anything to chance. I even hear a certain respect in his voice when he answers:

'Yes, madam, it is an *e*, Barraquer, the Barraquer Clinic. It's at the corner of Calle Montaner.'

He explains it all to her calmly and even draws a little map.
She asks for the telephone number.

'You'll find it easily.'

'Even more easily if you give it to me.'

'Of course.'

He calls the secretary back. Valushka's questions are precise,
essential, practical. All of her Slavic eccentricity seems to have
disappeared. She and the doctor are as thick as thieves now,
and I sense that if she asked him for the moon, he would try to
get it for her. She says later on:

'I trust him. He's a special kind of person, very sensitive,
very intuitive.'

This return to Russian logic reassures me.

In a small room, we watch the film of the operation.

Dr K. stays for more than half an hour describing the first
phase, but then his secretary calls him away. Valushka's comments are limited to 'How horrible!' Somewhat annoyed, I ask
her to tell me more. 'I don't know,' she says, 'I can't see
anything, there's blood everywhere.' Then, towards the end of
the film, I hear a strange sound in her throat.

'What's up?'

'It's dreadful. They're putting a kind of eggshell over the eye,
and there is an eye painted on it.'

'What did you say, an eggshell?'

'Don't ask . . . it's dreadful!'

Before leaving, I want some explanations. We slip into Dr K's
office between two patients.

'Excuse me, Doctor, what is that eggshell Valushka tells me
is put on or in the eye at the end of the operation?'

'Oh, it's just a plastic prosthesis to make the eyeball look
normal.'

Only then do I realise that, behind my eyelids, my eyes have
become two balls of raw meat. The almost phosphorescent
verdigris colour of the iris, the blackness of the pupil, and the
bluish whiteness of the cornea, that incredible combination of
hues, which in human beings is lovelier than the loveliest
enameled jewel, has been replaced by steak tartare, and this

makes me intensely sad. I had naïvely thought that behind my
eyelids, perhaps because I was able to perceive light, everything
was there, still intact. It reminds me of those cameras that as
a child I thought so beautiful only to be told they were not in
working order. It seemed to me that they were suffering from
some mysterious disease. But even if they were no longer of
any use, their power to fascinate and their magic were intact.
In a way, you still felt observed by this dead object.

Back on the street, with Valushka holding onto my arm, I am
no longer quite sure that I want to have my eyelids opened to
uncover that horror. I am not so sure I want to have that
monstrous thing, impaled by a tooth, peering from behind a
motionless, plastic façade. And all that in order to obtain a range
of vision no broader than a piece of confetti. I almost begin to
cherish my darkness and my eyes with their slightly Mongolian
look. I don't want to become an object of horror. For a tiny
patch of blue sky, I am not ready to jeopardise my relationship
with others. I have thought all too often of what my life would
have been like if I had not had the reflex to wash my face in cold
water, that is, to be blind and without a face, unable to see,
unable to be looked at, not wanting to be seen. In any case,
according to Dr K., there is only one eye that may be operated
on, the left one. It was supposed to be removed but has
apparently done better than the right, which has almost completely atrophied.

'A single eye is much better,' says Valushka. 'With a black
patch you'll look just like a pirate.'

'And you think that will go with the decoration of your living
room?'

She laughs and then suddenly becomes serious.

'You're going to see again. And after the operation, we'll
arrange to meet in a café, in New York or Paris. It'll be
extraordinary. You will see me, you will see my face, and I'll be
afraid that you won't like me. I want so much for you to see me,
to see my eyes. I'm not very good at using words. I am a dancer
and the only way I can truly express myself is through my eyes
and my gestures. Call Dr A. right away.'

TWENTY

On those sleepless nights, thinking of Valushka, of that hope rising in Barcelona, of that confrontation with the Minotaur, I listen to the tremendous roar of New York. The city rumbles and flashes like a meteor hurled into an aimless course. Mad and splendid. During these early days of June, windows are left open to the warm night, and every evening a woman, always the same one, can be heard having an orgasm. A strange and solitary singing in the heart of New York. Nothing to remind you of the gazelle of the Song of Songs, but, rather, of the clumsy hippopotamuses I have seen copulating in the backwaters of Africa. For some time now, a crazy bird has been singing every morning in the trees beneath my bedroom window. Every morning, at exactly at five o'clock, probably coming from Central Park, this little scatterbrain begins a series of mocking chortles, chirps, and wild snickering, as if he were jeering at all these sleeping human beings.

One night, the telephone rings around three o'clock and I hear Valushka's tearful voice. I don't really understand what has happened, but her despair seems as vast and monotonous as the Russian plain. I would like to console her, to go and take her in my arms, to 'cocoliner' her (to use a strange word she has concocted from the Italian). But I forgot to go to the bank today and cannot take a taxi.

I hang up without having been able to calm her. I am enraged by my helplessness, so imprisoned. Before, I would have run the thirty blocks between us, but tonight, sitting on this rug, I am bound by darkness. Suddenly, an inner voice tells me, 'I'm sure it is possible.' Struck by the enormity of the idea, I reject it. Going out on the street alone, I have never done it; and at three in the morning! 'That's just it,' the voice continues, 'at this hour there is less traffic, less noise, the air is thinner, and it will be easier to interpret the sounds.'

Questioning myself, I find the strength I need for this venture. I suddenly start to laugh with the realisation that this strength comes from love, from that wonderful feeling that projects one outside oneself just as I am being projected onto the street tonight.

The warm night touches my face, my hands. I stand still for a while, my long fibreglass cane held in front of me like a fencing foil ready for a duel with darkness. Immobile, I create a vacuum inside myself, become a nocturnal animal, a lithe black panther blending into the night. Sounds of emptiness echo from the neighbouring garage, drawing me in. I resist and follow a straight line. There's the bank whose glass walls form the corner of the street and Madison Avenue.

I cross the avenue, to the west side, which I know better, and calmly begin to walk uptown.

When my cane taps against the metal trapdoors that cover cellars under the sidewalk, I instinctively go around to avoid stepping on them. I hate anything that covers a void.

At one point, I stop without really knowing why; my brain is flashing the danger signal. I put my hand out slowly and, a foot from my face, touch a metal pole that my inexperienced cane had not detected. A few blocks later, I hear voices, laughter, and a radio. They are coming towards me. From the salsa music, I can tell that they are Puerto Ricans. They sound to me slightly drunk or stoned. In any case, it's too late to cross the street, and the worst thing would be to show my fear. I force myself to walk at a steady pace and to swing my cane from side to side in even arcs. My nerves are stretched to breaking point. A few yards from the group I hear the voices stop although the radio goes on. They must have seen me. They are silent as I pass by them, then a voice says:

'Hey, man!'

I answer:

'Hi! It's a lovely night.'

Another voice says:

'Yes, sir!'

But the tension has been so great that I have lost count of the streets. I don't know whether I'm at 72nd, 73rd, or 74th. The only thing to do is cross Madison again, and when I feel the rubber matting of the Hotel Carlyle under my feet I'll know that I'm between 76th and 77th. I walk faster and faster, with enthusiasm for this new-found freedom. In fact, I am covered with sweat and my hand grips the cane as if trying to graft it onto my palm. I force my fingers to relax and become aware of how much they hurt.

When I reach 92nd Street, I search for a phone booth and find one a block farther on. A sleepy voice tells me that she's much better, that she is sleeping, and that she will bring me some croissants in the morning.

This is perfectly all right with me, and anyhow the night is too exciting for me to be the least bit disappointed. Suddenly I hear Aho's voice: 'You thought the important thing was to go and comfort that woman! You are forgetting what old Abdul Jemal told you on the Flores Sea: of little importance is the port, it's the voyage that counts.' It is a long time since I have heard his voice and, as always, he reappears under extraordinary circumstances, as if the triviality of everyday life doesn't warrant disturbing his royal person. I hear his laughter. He is happy, and I am amused at the idea of Aho walking down Madison Avenue in full regalia, clad in his cloak with all the dignity of a Roman senator, presenting the incongruous sight of two feet gnarled like roots in his chieftain's sandals on the city asphalt.

An hour later, I throw myself down on my bed, exhausted and with my heart beating like a tom-tom. I calm down by listening to the last movement of Beethoven's Ninth, that hymn to life, conducted at a galloping pace by Furtwängler.

The next day, I tell Lesley about my sixty-block walk during the night. She doesn't seem to appreciate this feat.

'You're crazy! You can't do that sort of thing! You're not ready for it yet. Something terrible could happen. You should know better than anybody how dangerous New York is at night!'

She speaks slowly, seriously, and I sense as much from her

silence as from her words that she doesn't really understand, for obviously I haven't given her the key: Valushka.

One afternoon, while I am out walking with Michael, we decide to go and visit a painter friend of mine.

In a phone booth, I dial his number. A man comes up to me.

'Excuse me,' he says. 'I'm an opthalmologist. Are you wearing those glasses so that you can understand your friend better?'

Astonished, I answer.

'Certainly not. I don't see how they could help me do that.'

'But he is blind.'

'Really? Well, if he's blind, I'm in a hell of a mess.'

Suddenly I realise that, to dial the number, I have given my white cane to Michael. I burst out laughing. The doctor turns towards Michael and, staring into what he believes to be two dead eyes, asks him:

'Have you been like this for a long time?'

Michael is cool by nature; what's more, he is still suffering from glaucoma.

'Six months.'

'You poor fellow!'

I laugh harder and harder. Furious, the doctor attacks me with:

'Aren't you ashamed of yourself! Making fun of your friend's misfortune!'

And we leave him standing there, unable to figure out whether I am guiding Michael or he is guiding me.

Today, after five hours of class, I am exhausted and skip piano practice. I phone Désirée, who doesn't answer, and decide to go home on my own.

The critical moment comes when I pass through the door that separates two worlds: the protected one of the Lighthouse and the normal one out on the street. On the line of this threshold there is a moment of pure fear, such as one knows before jumping from a high dive.

— 59th Street. I missed the little iron fence around the tree in front of the Lighthouse, which normally helps me to find my bearings when I practise with Lesley. The noise is deafening. The intersection at 59th Street and Lexington must be the busiest in the world. Though I have missed the fence, I recognise the pole from which flags are hung. It's like an old friend putting me in the right direction. The crowd jostles me and my cane gets entangled among various legs. About ten yards farther on, I pass the florist whose sidewalk flower pots attract several hundred canes a day. This shopkeeper is one of the rare people I have met who have no compassion whatsoever for the blind. The smell of coffee and fried eggs – that's the coffee shop, with its door that swings out and will hit you if you're not careful. And finally, here's the tobacco shop, whose aroma tells me that I should turn up Park Avenue. I decide to cheat, following the building's wall with my cane, which is not the method we were taught.

– 60th Street. I cross over without any trouble, listening to the traffic. A voice shouts at me, 'The show's over!' What does that mean? I am behind the curtain of the theatre. The show is over; I have drifted into the wings. I now see the world with its stage sets, its ropes and pulleys. Does he take me for an actor who would like to continue the performance on the street? In any event, the curtain has fallen. Darkness has set in and the show is definitely over.

I am now walking without touching the wall because of the iron grillwork and I have to swing my cane from side to side. I find the tapping of the cane unbearable. I move forward like a crab.

– 61st Street. A woman in a fur coat helps me cross. She is extremely tall and I tell her so. No answer.

– 62nd Street. I must have veered to one side and left the crosswalk, because I run into a car. A man warns me, 'Watch out! You're off course.' He joins me. 'I am a doctor and I was watching you. You're not managing very well. You're a good forty-five degrees off.' I don't say anything, but it seems to me that forty-five degrees isn't bad for a beginner.

– 63rd Street. I ask for help because of the excavations for a new subway line.

– 64th Street. Con Edison is at work, probably for the city

heating system. Three pneumatic drills explode in my ears and completely disorientate me. I don't have long to wait before someone pushes his elbow in my hand. No word is spoken except for my 'Thank you' on the other side of the street. I continue but pay twice as much attention, because it's only my ear that will let me know when I have reached my destination. At last, over my head I hear the canopy of my building. I am home. I find myself crying from sheer emotion – neither joy nor sadness, just emotion. And I am crying also because I am more acutely aware than ever of being blind.

When I think back over that first time alone in daytime traffic, it seems to me that both my eyes were there. My brain saw the pole, the flowers, the grillwork, the fur coat. It is an illusion, but the truth is that my memory of the visible world is intact.

This is confirmed when I show a friend from France around New York: the World Trade Center, Chinatown, Little Italy, Greenwich Village. I remember everything. I know how to find my way around and can guide her.

I make her stop in front of certain shop windows that had impressed me, like the one in Chinatown where there's a chicken that dances for a quarter.

And then there's the window of a travel agency dating from the fifties in which a faded seascape in the background, a cardboard palm tree, a beach chair, a straw hat, and dark glasses invite you to the tropics. But, with the passage of years, a thick layer of grey dust has covered everything.

And there's also that window on Mott Street where San Gennaro, the Neapolitan saint, slightly mafioso, sparkles with gold and precious stones.

And that trompe-l'oeil painting of a bakery with all kinds of wonderful loaves of bread that they don't make anymore.

Mercer Street, Centre Street, SoHo. We pass in front of a gallery where I know one of my paintings is being held on consignment. I feel an irresistible urge to see it again. We go in, but things don't go too well. The gallery owner tells me:

'If this is your idea of a joke, it's a lousy one! Get the hell out of here!'

I get angry. My friend tries to calm me down.

'You know, he has a point. It must seem strange for someone who is blind to ask to see a painting.'

I insist:

'It's a picture I painted myself!' But I realise I am compounding the misunderstanding and suspect that I'm going to get a kick in the ass.

Finally everything works out, except for the fact that on the painting's smooth surface, my fingers see nothing. Only my memory . . .

Tonight I went to a theatre for the handicapped near Canal Street and Broadway. I have been turning down their invitations for two months.

Rick, the director, asks his cast to express an emotion – just any emotion – by sounds. In a few minutes, the whole theatre begins to reverberate. They are like drums, echoing each other's emotions, vibrating with each other's inner resonance. The sounds bounce back and forth and sometimes come together in a chorus. Certain shouts are picked up and answered first by one person, then another, then still another. . . . Very little joyful emotion, much suffering, anger, despair. No sound of laughter or joyous exclamations. Sorrow, sadness, despondency.

A man blinded in an accident shouts:

'Why me? Why me?'

This infernal frenzy gets louder and louder and then dies down. It becomes unbearable for me. So unbearable that I concentrate my inner gaze on Valushka's face.

On stage, there are eight paraplegics in wheelchairs, as well as two blind people and three who are mentally retarded. They have such courage, such guts! Some of the paraplegics live more than an hour away and do their own driving. When they leave, I listen to the sound of their cars starting up and can't help thinking that, in spite of all that courage, they're not going to have a very big slice of life's cake. Two of them, nevertheless, have married.

Rick tells me their story. They were left alone one night in the same hospital room. Making use of whatever pieces of furniture and equipment they could find there, they managed to pull themselves out of their wheelchairs and to come together in an embrace on the floor, where they were found in the morning. And in my head I visualise these two bodies, dead from the waist down, crawling towards each other and caressing. And I think of the wild, tender, harmonious dance of two normal beings who are drawn towards each other. A revelation of our own animal beauty. What became, that night, of this revelation, of this dance of love?

My next mobility lesson with Lesley is a real disaster. I have never functioned so badly. Lost, zigzagging, exposing myself to danger, walking in front of oncoming cars, running into buses. Terrible! Lesley sends me home.

I want to go home by myself so that the day will not be a complete defeat. Someone catches hold of me and draws me off to the side because I was approaching an open trapdoor. I had not detected it with my cane, and I find myself now in a cold sweat. Lesley has warned me how many blind people have been swallowed up by those traps.

In spite of its dangers, the street attracts me and I seize every opportunity to avoid taking the familiar routes. I walk down Madison going from drugstore to drugstore looking for a pink hot-water bottle. Valushka has a stomach ache and dreams of having a pink hot-water bottle. I don't find any and sense, somehow, that these druggists disapprove. Why does a blind man want a pink hot-water bottle? Green, blue, yellow, but not a single pink one. Someone produces a red one that is 'kind of pink,' but his voice tells me it is really red.

One day, the directors of the Lighthouse get us all together and ask what each of us thinks of the centre. Requests come flying thick and fast: a swimming pool, a bowling alley, and something I find astonishing – colour television.

At one point, the director turns to me:

'What does our young Frenchman have to say?'

'The Lighthouse is not perfect, far from it, and it's important for it to stay that way! The more uncomfortable it is, the better.'

'What do you mean?'

'This way we'll feel more eager to get back to the outside world.'

Some of these people have taken root here. One of them comes to see me in the music studio, where I am practising scales.

'I've come to ask you to help us with our petition to get better pianos and more competent teachers.'

He is about my age and has been coming here for eleven years. I reply:

'I won't lift a finger to improve the Lighthouse. I have some good advice to give you. Get the hell out of here! Go back onto the street, the sooner the better!'

Only once did I take the initiative. I heard there was a wonderful swimming pool in the basement that was never used. Why? No one knew. So I went to see the counsellor in charge of sports.

'I'm sorry, but we don't have a swimming instructor.'

Why let that stop us? Two days later, I came back with Bob, the brother of a friend of mine, who had won a gold medal for lifesaving last year in Miami. In addition, he was offering his services for practically nothing.

The counsellor asked him, 'Do you know how to make pottery?' Taken aback, Bob confessed his inadequacy in that department. So the swimming pool remained closed because the budget required that the same person teach both swimming and pottery. Disgusted, I threatened to organise a demonstration, with people carrying signs in Braille.

In any case, Braille, instructors, canes, dogs, and blind people, they can all go and take a running jump. My only hope is Barcelona.

TWENTY-ONE

Ten years ago, while passing through Barcelona, I stopped by a little restaurant in a working-class suburb where I was told that the local speciality was grilled sheep's head. I now remember, with a certain queasiness, that split skull staring at me from my plate with its two protruding, dead eyes.

I am the guest of an important woman of Barcelona, the head of B. Industries. As it happens, my hostess isn't in town and it's her secretary who comes to pick me up at the airport and take me to an apartment in the residential district.

Although it's mid-August, the air is fresh. The apartment has a particular odour, similar to that of Italian homes; it's not a matter of olive oil, garlic, or cooking, but, rather, a scent of wax and mothballs, of a house that is well looked after. On the balcony, Barcelona smells different from New York or Paris. Cities have different odours, just as they have different mentalities, different architectures, different attitudes.

My appointment with Dr A. is for tomorrow.

I am obsessed with this and, at the same time, I am irritated to be forced to have to think of nothing but my blindness. It is impossible to listen to music or read the fifteen cassettes of 'The Voyages of Ibn-Batouta', the Arab who went travelling in the area of Makassar in the fourteenth century.

I am preoccupied by the condition of my left eye. What are the tests going to show? And, above all, what will this new vision be like? I think of that plastic eggshell covering a hideous, bloody eyeball, with that implanted tooth. I think of the whole poetic and romantic heritage associated with a loving look; eyes lost in eyes; out of sight, out of mind. What becomes of a loving look when there is only a layer of plastic with a little hole in the middle? What can one read there?

In the plane, there were two women talking about a young man. 'He has such beautiful eyes, and when he looks at me, it makes me feel like . . .' Tunnel vision, Dr K. had said. And that tooth, just what it takes to cast a piercing look, no doubt.

I wake up the next morning with my head full of terrifying dreams. I don't remember them very clearly. I only know that it concerns my eyes, something about my eyes having been opened up surgically, but I cannot see. And yet, when I look in a mirror, I see my blind eyes. To forget, I turn on the radio. The first music I hear is Arabic, which seems perfectly natural. I change stations and discover some very beautiful liturgical chants. Then the Vatican broadcast, which is much clearer than in France. Religious Spain must have installed a powerful relay station. At six o'clock, the news: bombs, assassination attempts, two civilian guards killed, Basque terrorists. And it's rounded off by César Franck's funereal symphony, slightly austere for the early morning. In any other city they'd be playing Mozart or some cheerful chamber music to start the day.

My hostess is still away. Apparently, she has retired for the hot season to a valley in the Pyrenees where she looks after her marvellous gardens. Antonio, one of her sons, accompanies me to the Barraquer Clinic on this Thursday morning.

The hall is immense, grey, white, and black; Velásquez's colours, only the pink is missing. The colour scheme ties the building to the 1940s; its fascist architecture is heavy, solemn. Under a cupola, half-mutilated Greek and Roman statues look down indifferently upon a tempestuous sea of Mediterranean faces. The hall is filled with a swarthy, guttural, restless crowd. Arabs, Greeks, Spaniards, some myopic, some presbyopic, others blind. The atmosphere is that of a bazaar, with all the hubbub of a drunken ship. Not very reassuring. It sounds like a factory and smells of money. To add to the confusion, barely audible insipid music sputters out through overhead loud-speakers. My legs are hit by a stick wielded by one of a group of blind Saudi Arabians who are frantically clearing the way for themselves as if rushing up to kiss the Kaaba. Yesterday or the day before, a Swede was stabbed on the steps. Was this son of the North eliminated by a mob from Asia Minor or by some Maltese who wanted gold frames for his glasses? Jostled, deafened, and disconcerted by the disorder in what was supposed to be a calm, serene temple of Hope, I arrive before the receptionist slightly drunk with noise and expectation. My heart beats wildly. This is it! I am going to see him, the great wizard. I am in the miraculous grotto, and I suddenly realise the commotion outside is really quite understandable, for all these people are as anxious as I. That's what I tell myself in my heart of hearts, ignoring the fact that ten other doctors also practise in this clinic. The woman behind the desk leafs through a large appointment book, then makes a phone call, and finally declares:

'No, Monsieur de Montalembert, you do not have an appointment with Dr A.'

'Yes, I do. I've had an appointment with Dr A. for two and a half months. I haven't crossed the Atlantic Ocean and all of Spain just to drop in on him.'

Antonio and the receptionist begin a dialogue in such rapid Spanish that it is incomprehensible to me. They are going to be at each other's throat any moment now. But everything ends up with 'Muy bien . . . gracias . . . con gusto . . .' and we are shown into a small windowless anteroom filled with the acrid smells of black cigarettes, stale cigars, and squalling children, whose mothers give them onions to suck.

We wait there for three hours on our feet, since all the seats are taken. At regular intervals, a door opens and Dr A.'s nurse calls out:

'Señor Eduardo Ramirez' or 'Señora Rosita Audegaar' or 'Señor Ahmed Choukri.'

After three hours, infuriated, I am convinced that all these people are perfectly well and are just wasting my great wizard's precious time. For whatever ails them, any old doctor would do. I turn to Antonio for confirmation.

'No, they can all see. Some of them have very thick glasses on.'

During these three hours, something rises up in me that is neither fear nor anguish, though resembling them both deeply. It is hope. I am going to see again. I know it.

Now that I am finally at the feet of the master and the process has begun, I have and will go on having all the patience in the world. At last my luck is going to turn. Soon, we are going to size up the beast and prepare for the corrida; the bull will be vanquished with one final thrust, the banderillas of darkness will be torn out of my flesh.

The room is now empty, and I have all the chairs on which to rest my hope.

'Señor de Montalembert.'

I get up and take a step. The nurse seizes my cane and my forearm, pulls, pushes, bumps me up against the door, and finally folds me onto a moleskin chair by pressing down on my shoulders. I am slightly indignant at being handled so brusquely but have no time to think about it, for Dr A.'s gruff voice is already addressing me.

'You did not have an appointment.'

'Yes, I did, I phoned you, or rather, Mrs N. phoned you at the beginning of June and I spoke to you myself. I also sent you my complete file, just as you asked me to.'

'That's not true! I wasn't here at the beginning of June; I was on vacation. We've looked for your file but we don't have it.'

I am taken aback and feel myself turning cold. Hasn't he just called me a liar? Something is wrong between this man and me. I feel it in the air, but I don't quite know what it is.

'Why do you wear those awful glasses? They're melodramatic and unnecessary. You must take them off; they're appalling.'

As I have said, I am prepared to be the most patient person in the world. This is no time for anger. I want you, Dr A., because you are the best and in spite of your rudeness I have confidence in you. You are the mechanic who can repair this damage, and that's all that counts. I explain things calmly, taking off my glasses:

'I feel comfortable behind them, protected. In fact, Doctor, I have not come all the way across the Atlantic to talk about my glasses, but about what's behind them.'

'All right, all right, if you feel comfortable with them, but aesthetically speaking, they are terrible. Put your head here.'

And his fingers, which are as gentle as his voice is rough, guide my face into the steel-and-plastic apparatus on his desk. He presses, scrutinises, explores, floods my eyes with light, scribbles nervously, mumbles some words in Spanish that I don't understand, and presses again.

'You can put your head back now.'

He comes around the desk and sits next to me. Turning on a small penlight, he asks me to indicate what direction the light is coming from. I am incapable and yet sense how important this is. I must at all costs get myself onto his operating table. So I invent answers at random, trying to catch any sound his hand may make on the penlight, but he must guess what I am up to, for I hear nothing.

'And now?'

'There!'

And my finger points into the void.

He sits back down at his desk.

'Señor de Montalembert, you are going to undergo a series of tests and I will see you again later this afternoon.'

So that's that. It's over! I leave his office with the impression that nothing has really begun. Why this animosity? I feel depressed but hide my disappointment. A nurse asks me to follow him.

'Go have lunch,' I tell Antonio. 'We'll get together later.'

The nurse takes me through various rooms to the basement. He walks quickly and silently, saying only, 'Más de prisa. Faster!' What a remarkable clinic – they make the blind gallop even before restoring their sight. I find myself sitting on a revolving stool, not knowing why I'm there, when a flash surprises me, flooding my brain with white light and rattling my nerves. Two photos are taken, one in profile, and we move into another room. After this penal formality, I almost expect to hear the cell door closing, but instead we again start playing the little game of 'Tell me what direction the light is coming from.' I cheat as best I can, although I'm not fooling anyone. An instrument is applied to my left eye, without explanation, perhaps to measure its pressure. All of that is done rapidly, automatically. The man's voice is expressionless; he is in a hurry, indifferent. Eventually, walking like a robot, he takes me back to a small waiting room, deserted and silent, next to the great cupola. For several hours I've felt that I have lost control of my existence, caught up by a wave, and that every decision has been made by the wave itself. In this waiting room, I keep reminding myself that there is nothing to understand; I must carry on. It seems to me that I have been in Barcelona for centuries, perhaps even that I was born here, that my life has consisted, and still only consists, of waiting, descending, ascending, waiting. Time passes slowly, as if a needle were caught in the spirals at the end of a record. I hear Apollinaire murmuring to me, 'How slow is life and how violent hope.'

Antonio has come back and is telling me about Spain, the king, the death of Franco, and Catalonia's parliamentary elections. I listen distractedly.

'Ahora, España es una casa de putas!'

He must be pro-Franco and yet he's not even thirty years old. But, as he goes on, a commotion in the large hall suddenly captures my attention. I hear someone shouting impatiently:

'Dónde? Pero dónde?'

And other voices:

'Señora, sígame Usted, por favor. . . .'

That voice . . . No, I must be mistaken. But I feel a warmth in this piece of stone that I have become, and before I'm sure of what's happening, my hands are touching you through your cotton dress, your ballerina's thighs, and suddenly I'm holding you and you're whispering:

'At last! You're here, I knew you were here.'

And clinging to each other, we catch our breath as if we were on the edge of a dark abyss.

She has rushed into the clinic like a meteor, demanding to see me without a moment's delay, shouting my name, becoming indignant when no one seems to know it, bursting into Dr A.'s office, moving through the underground rooms like a shooting star. In fact, 'for good luck,' she is wearing her dress with moons and comets on it. She makes me touch her hair, which she has braided across her temples and joined at the nape of her neck. Our hands are held together so tightly that the lines of our palms are interwoven, blended, melded, until they become one, and I realise that the lines of our lives are following the same scar.

'I have left everything, I have come to be yours.'

I am afraid she will detect how desperate I have become. She senses a distance between us, grows impatient, and goes off to look for a Coca-Cola.

'How beautiful she is!' says Antonio, whom I had forgotten about.

Now that she is here, everything is going to work out. I walk towards Dr A.'s office with confidence. As we pass through the hall, Valushka says:

'How strange for a clinic to display all those mutilated statues! I don't like it!'

I feel that it really does disturb her.

The doctor's voice, softer when he greets Valushka, grows harsh again when he addresses me:

'I think . . . Please understand, you must listen carefully to every word I say. I don't think anything can be done. Perhaps your left eye . . . perhaps. To be absolutely certain, to form a definite opinion, I must open it up. There is, I think, atrophy of the eyeballs. You have a good perception of light but very poor projection; you aren't able to locate the light, which indicates that the retina is in bad shape. Because of both the atrophy and the poor projection, I don't think I'll be able to do anything, but I have to operate to be sure.'

Atrophy, my eyes like two little shoe buttons. The verdict affects me like a new ice age. My luck hasn't turned. The prognosis is bad. Standing before the great doctor and Valushka, I am almost ashamed of the pitiful state of my eyes. Her voice, almost tender, asserts:

'But doctor, you are going to do something!'

'Madam,' and his voice becomes gentle again, 'I am the best in the world for this particular operation. The state of Monsieur de Montalembert's eyes is not good at all. I believe, you understand, I believe there is atrophy. I must open them up to be certain.' Then, turning to me: 'Come back Monday morning at nine o'clock, without having eaten, and I will operate on you.'

'The surgeon who operated on me in New York gave strict orders that my eyes were not to be touched for two years; that is, for another few months. He said the eye must be given time to heal and stabilise. That's why he sewed the eyelids and . . .'

'Ridiculous! When were you operated on? More than a year ago! And you imagine that everything has healed in that time? No! If he sewed your eyelids, it was to hide the shit, like putting a diaper on a baby's bottom.'

There's a comforting image!

'And anyway, if you don't want me to operate, I don't understand what you came here for. You're wasting my time!'

'I came to consult you and to make an appointment to be operated on, but not now.'

'You want to come back! You must have money to burn.'

My nerves have just about had it and I am barely aware that tears are rolling down my cheeks. Valushka tells me about this later. She tries to placate the doctor:

'But, Doctor, can he come back?'

'Whenever he likes, but it's a waste of time. In three days, if you want, I will operate and he will know right away how things stand.'

'Thank you, Doctor, but if it's not to be in three days, let's set another date right now.'

'Fine. Do you have a particular date in mind?'

'Yes. February 23.'

I sense that her prompt reply surprises him. As he writes the date in his appointment book, I smile to myself. February 23 is Valushka's birthday.

The doctor gets up, comes over to me, and pulls back my lips with his thumb to examine my teeth. I remain motionless, like an animal at a fair, because however roughly he treats me, he is still my only hope. If there were really no chance at all of recovering my vision, he wouldn't go to the trouble of examining my teeth. Nevertheless, I don't want him to operate now and risk ruining everything. Perhaps also, deep down, I'm afraid of the verdict, and in this way I prolong the hope.

As we leave, Valushka says:

'He's an extraordinary man. I have complete confidence in him. You'll see!'

I don't dare ask her to clear up this last ambiguity.

TWENTY-TWO

We move into the Colón Hotel in the heart of the old Gothic quarter, just under the cathedral, not Gaudí's but the earlier one. The Colón is one of those small, forgotten, once luxurious hotels dating from the late nineteenth century in which everything is red, black, and gold. The personnel and the velvet upholstery smell of cigarillos, Celta, and dust. The balcony of the bedroom overlooks the square, where children play. Under this window a horse passes back and forth ominously at regular intervals. I don't like the sound of its hooves on the pavement; it has that weary sound of horses drawing a hearse.

'I have left everything, I have come to be yours.' I can feel all your expectation. For you this day is a dawn, and I try to conceal my exhaustion, my tarnished hope, and my desire to sink into a coma, huddled over my wound. Your nails clutch a love gone into solitude. So I lean over you and feebly between our hands light is rekindled. Planets tumble from your hair. Constellations dance around us; comets fall; and from the earth we free ourselves. Your lips spit out stars. In order not to wake the neighbours, we muffle laughter and tears under the pillows. The cathedral bells ring out the hours, counting the quarters, decanting the time; sharp and bitter like hemlock on the quarter, dull and cracked on the hour. And this horse going back and forth, filling me with dread.

One night, an orchestra came to play a Beethoven symphony, and fireworks lit up the cathedral. You didn't even bother to go onto the balcony to see what I couldn't see. And if I had met you earlier, in New York, when I had those premonitions, you would have saved me and I would have taken you off to a house by the sea, where I could paint and be with you. 'Don't hurt us!'

With that biting humour of yours, that night you told me, 'In your situation, I don't understand why you don't commit suicide,' and that idea made us laugh, because we were so happy to be alive, so enchanted with each other, tired with joy and scented with the same sweat. I give you birth and you give me back my childhood.

In the light of our love, lucidity slowly becomes a wound. Twang . . . God, how cracked that bell! As cracked as a dream falling apart. And with the passing hours, you bump against the absence of my sight. With your Russian logic, you thought that with time your kisses would unsolder my eyelids and that at last my sight would penetrate you. The horse tramples my heart, which echoes the tolling of the bells.

In this black labyrinth, you have come with the dazzling light of your hair, a golden halo. The dark, twisting tunnels, so endlessly bewildering, have become crystalline, and the menace of the Minotaur has vanished. The monstrous beast crouching at the heart of darkness has emerged from the shadows, blind and vicious, backed up against the wall, like a body gone limp, a viscous shade assassinated by light. And the labyrinth has exploded into galaxies echoing into the infinite. You have released in me the music of all musics and within us arises the thunderous cathedral of poetry's plain song. Already my heart is being torn from my side by a wound that I choose to ignore. Already my heart is deserting me for you, is betraying me. My veins like tentacles melt with yours, and our bloods become one. I enter you as I enter myself and the miracle is accomplished. Explode the walls with the guts of the beast! Then I sail to the shore of that secret garden that I cannot reach. Foams of sweat cover me, falling like diamond rain on you as you lie, waiting, timeless, offered, open but not given. And indeed that nuance is important to me.

At that instant amorphous flies appear, so heavy that they cannot fly higher than our heads, circling like black thoughts. I suspect them of feeding on the snot of that funereal horse passing to and fro under the window. August rots Barcelona; only the evening breeze brings onto the square a band that plays fandangos. And this music, which speaks to us of youth, leaves us ripped apart. Like a wild stallion, I gallop to the heart of your self to erase the distance I sense in your unyielding gaze. You came into that darkness where you knew you would find me: the horror fascinates you, chills you, and now you refuse to let it enter the garden. No longer will one of your gestures show me the way, and the slowly flowing sand of time buries my heart, which suffocates at the approach of your departure. The farther I sink into you, the more violently I tear you apart, bite your sex, rip myself on your breasts sharpened by love. Gently I feel your legs closing above me. For a moment the distance in your eyes diminishes, sin engulfs you, and there you lie like a fallen star. You take me by the hand and slowly open the heavy door behind which the long horses of my dreams are hanging, skinned, from iron hooks. You look in silence.

Dogs bite each other on the piazza. The night is torrid. At the break of dawn, we listen to cars feverishly starting up and driving off. And here you are, so naked and beautiful; and the garden like a mirage fades away.

Sulphur, blood, and sperm roar in my veins, and my courage is broken by the tetanising erection which paralyses me, soldering my bones, twisting my muscles, and blocking my lungs. There at the threshold of the garden, I am unable to enter. How your dark eyes look at me! But you remain a stranger and I cannot read your thoughts. From deep within you there rises that vapour of sadness which, like certain poisons, finds its strength in its tenuous subtlety.

Later you confessed, 'I was so eager for you to tell me "Let's go," for you to take me along. But you couldn't, and I was hurt.' Only once did we leave that room with the impression of digging ourselves out of quicksand. In a state of hallucination, we go down into the dining room of the old hotel. In your voice I hear your departure. And suddenly the pain becomes so sharp that I fall. I fall into an even blacker blackness. My eyes try desperately to fix onto something but there is only blackness. I slip into the distance; my inner sight cannot focus on anything. I am trapped in the very act of fainting. There is no escape. There is nothing now but the void into which I am falling. Death must be that.

I fall off my chair. You pick me up, and I take hold of myself quickly so that you won't be frightened. You have not shown your fear but you have seen my weakness.

You said later, 'In Barcelona, I felt something so great for you growing within me. We were so sensitive to everything that I needed your strength.'

You are lying now like a wounded animal on my bed. You are going to leave. From your eyes emerges arctic music in this aurora borealis.

'You are on the path now, I see the path, I see it.'

But I think: Even if I get my sight back, I know very well, deep down, that I am no longer the same. Along with my eyes, I have lost my innocence. With the tip of her finger she puts salve on my eyes, which are burning, and touches the left one.

'It is more swollen than the other one – I mean, there is more of an eyeball there. It will see again.'

It was the last time she was to touch my body. Since we are due never to see each other again.

We do not say good-bye to each other. Instinctively I press my finger on her lips so that nothing will be said. She understands, gets up in silence, opens the door; I feel her breath upon me, if it's not a draft between the hallway and the window. There is a moment of prolonged silence and the air is once again still.

The present has just closed and already the past on the other side of that door is walking away, while in the room I advance backward towards the future.

Time rings out from the cathedral, indifferent. It is four o'clock. A solitary child plays with a ball. It's Sunday afternoon; the siesta has been longer than usual.

And very soon it is six o'clock. I wait for something even though I know that nothing will happen. I am bored, in pain. Despair seeps in with the same slowness as the sun setting in the sky I cannot see. As this afternoon dies away, the horse's steps became heavier and the harness bells less resonant, like my soul. I take a sip of red wine, this Catalonian wine as thick as opium. My night seems interminable. Already through the window the wind is becoming fresher. Warm and slow, evening arrives with its orchestras and the music that hurts. My shadow guided me towards you and you led me to the light but the light was coming from you. This evening, night closes its claws on me. I am a prisoner, and on the walls flows the green sweat of this night that refuses to end. In the depths of the labyrinth, the Minotaur glows, black and red.

Freed from your scrutinising gaze, I return to the dimension of the imaginary and give in to the temptation of the invisible.

TWENTY-THREE

'No, I cannot recommend this operation; you are taking an unnecessary risk that may ruin your chances for the future. In the first place, the optic nerve could be damaged. Prostho-keratoplasty and odonto-keratoprosthesis are discoveries of the sixties that were refined in the seventies. So they are operations that are twenty years old. At this moment, you have researchers working around the world to find new techniques, one of which could be more appropriate to your case. It seems to me that it would be better to wait for these operating techniques to be improved, rather than to go and risk your future in Barcelona.'

With these words Dr T. refuses my request for a letter to the Crime Victims Compensation Board to recommend the operation. Twelve thousand dollars, I must find twelve thousand dollars, the fee charged by the Barraquer Clinic for Dr A.'s operation. Twelve thousand dollars to regain my sight. I'm not worried. I'll find it, even if I need to rob a bank.

The Crime Victims organisation was hesitant. 'Why Barcelona? Why go to Spain, when we have excellent surgeons in the United States? Have Dr T. send us a letter specifying that the operation can be performed only by this Dr A. of Barcelona and we will study the case.' And now Dr T., guided by his conscience, refuses to help me to pursue my dreams. He speaks of risk, whereas I think only of hope.

I return home feeling disturbed because his tone is so categorical. And what if, in my impatience, I really were to jeopardise my future? Doubt has crept in and I don't know where to turn for advice. The fear of doing something irreparable gives me insomnia. I telephone Dr K.

'I can't make the decision for you; only you can do it. The

only thing I can tell you is that Dr T. has probably not seen Dr A. operate. He probably saw other doctors operating, it's often a bloody and messy job. Dr A. is thirty-six, he is a genius and his operations are highly precise. I can tell you that much, but the decision is still entirely up to you.'

The crisis lasts a few more days, until I convince myself that the question is not so much medical as philosophical. I am trying to obtain results, that is, to be able to see again, at least partially. Dr T.'s opposition comes from the fact that doing so involves a risk. But if I look back over my life, every step forward has always involved some risk, and in this case it will be a calculated one. If the operation fails, the chances of my ever being able to see again may be ruined. But what is important to me is having my sight back at thirty-six, not seventy. I will go to Barcelona.

Once this decision is made, I feel calm and strong. At the same time I decide, since Valushka has disappeared, to have this operation in solitude. That way, whatever the result may be, I will be able to accept it without being surrounded by useless compassion or pity, and also without being obliged to console anyone. Altogether, in this situation, it's better to be alone.

I will go see the budget officer of Crime Victims; I will go to the headquarters of this organisation, to Albany if necessary. I will pour out all my hopes on his desk, and I'll be very surprised if he denies my request.

Since Barcelona, since the light of hope began to grow in me, it is increasingly difficult to tolerate the atmosphere at the Lighthouse. Out of discipline, through sheer love of the game, and also because of my affection for Lesley, I continue to attend mobility classes almost regularly. In any case, Mr Scholtz has notified me that I am reaching the end of my training. I know how to sew on a button, tell whether my socks are inside out or not; I have become a skilful typist and read contracted Braille fluently. The state of New York, which has been paying for this education, sends two commissioners to check on the results and to question me about my future plans. They find it inadmissible that I live alone. I am blind, handicapped, obliged to depend on others.

'In your case, Monsieur de Montalembert, you ought to find a nice girl.'

Civil servants or pimps? They laugh at my indignation and give me a lecture on love and need.

Today I will not go to the Lighthouse. After a series of sleepless nights, I might find myself aimlessly wandering around the streets. My head is spinning. To keep myself occupied, I am making Braille labels for my records when the phone rings. I recognise the voice: it is Dwike, the Voodoo priest from Harlem. He has just read the article I published with a journalist from the *New York Times* in their *Sunday Magazine*, 'Voodoo in Harlem.' And yet I had insisted that my name should not be mentioned, since I wasn't sure if I wanted to resume contact with this religion, which has veered away from the paths of Aho. Slavery has made Voodoo a religion of defence and attack. To ward off whips and rifles, all they had was the Voodoos they carried within them. And that is how this religion of harmony, of cosmic dance, became a religion of combat. One had to become invulnerable to bullets, throw the evil master into madness, and win love, which makes the soul gentle. That explains why people in general, and the *New York Times* journalists in particular, are absolutely set on linking my mugging to my activities in Harlem. The first journalist sent to me by the *New York Times* would not listen to reason, so I refused to collaborate with him. The second, who had been forewarned, pretended to believe everything I said, but I could hear in his voice that he was lying. I sent him away. Finally, the third one, young, idealistic, and decorated with a Ph.D in comparative religions, struck me as sincere and we did the article.

'Very good! Very good article, man! All of Harlem has read it. It's a good job.'

Dwike's voice is enthusiastic. Ten pages in the *Times Sunday Magazine* . . .

'It's fantastic publicity!' he says, echoing the kind of business vocabulary that even heads of congregations use in the United

States. 'But I thought you had gone back to Europe. We hadn't heard anything about you.'

'No, I'm still in New York but I had an accident. I was mugged, I got acid in my eyes. I'm blind.'

'Shit, man! What do you mean, you can see nothing?'

'No, I can't see anything anymore.'

'Shit! Incredible! You've got to explain it all to me. Perhaps there was something . . . I mean, I feel responsible. Can I come over now?'

'Now . . . Yes, of course.'

Half an hour later, Dwike is here, firing questions like a machine gun. He has come with Alicia, who doesn't say a word. I sense that she is distressed. I tell them about the mugging.

'The fucking bastards,' interrupts Dwike. 'Why didn't you call us? We would have found them, and, man, you know . . . I've got to understand, man, I've got to understand. My responsibility is at stake, my reputation uptown. What about your Legba?'

'I threw it into the sea so that it would be at peace, as I was taught in Africa. Only the sea can defuse it.'

'I know, I know. It's OK. Why do you live alone? It's no good. Come to live with us. I own some buildings. I'll give you an apartment, man. You won't have to bother about anything.'

I know that he is sincere and that, surrounded by their friendship and the sense of community that is peculiar to Harlem, I'll have nothing to worry about. But I laugh when I think of the reaction of my friends, of the New York State social workers, and of the Crime Victims Compensation Board if they were to learn that I had moved once again to live in Harlem.

New York softens in the waning summer. Sometimes a cold wind blows down the avenues, announcing the season when you come closer to those you love. That season when the slightest breeze makes the heart shiver, when you curl yourself up with love. Under the fading sky, I march along the avenues, cross the streets, and breathe in the air a desire and at the same time a stench of carrion under the dead leaves of my love. I mustn't think about Valushka, and all I do is think about her. I have nothing to say to anyone. I must be left to my haunting memories,

my obsession with hope and love. I walk because the forced
concentration of this act prevents my brain from spinning like a
top. I walk in order not to go mad. A hand is placed on my arm
and I am immobilised. My veins empty. A hand slips over my
wrist. For an instant I recognise her hand; no, not her hand,
but her touch. And now I recover my breath, because I have
made a mistake. It isn't the scent of tuberose that fills my
nostrils, but another that is unknown to me.

'Who is it?'

There is no answer except for a slight pressure on my wrist.
My heart, which has no nose, jumps. I try to reason with it:
'No, it's not her scent.'

'Tell me, who are you?'

I free my hand, and my fingers move up her arm to plunge
into the golden cloud just as she says:

'It's me.'

'But how can you have changed your perfume without letting
me know?' I say stupidly, as if we had been seeing each other
every day.

Sitting opposite me on the rug, she asks me questions. She is
indignant at Dr T.'s refusal.

'So what are you going to do?'

'I'll figure something out.'

'It's scandalous! You don't need those worries on top of
everything else. You should go to Barcelona with an absolutely
free mind.'

She announces that she is going to go back to the Island next
year, towards June. As always when someone talks to me about
the Island, images spring up without my being able to stop them.
And I attempt to share them with Valushka. At one point, I ask
her a question. Not getting an answer, I stretch out my hand to
where I know she is sitting. There is only emptiness. A doubt.
Yet on the rug I touch a camera and some records. I call her.
No answer. I look for her body on the rug, then on the chairs,
the piano bench, then in every corner, even in the bathtub. I
have the impression of being spied upon. I listen, trying to hear
her breathing, and wonder if she is watching me listening for

her. The door is closed and I haven't heard it either open or shut. Gradually her presence evaporates, she is no longer there. And I undergo the metamorphosis from a seen being to an unseen being. I go back to the scattered objects she has left behind and among them I find a book that I had missed. I try to understand the reason for such a cruel act. The records are new, still unopened. I can feel her distress without being able to understand it. This brutal solitude, which has come upon me at an indeterminate moment, leaves me with an uncomfortable feeling. Unbearable – that moment when absent to myself, I existed only through her eyes, which were no longer there.

That feeling is so nauseating that I must go out immediately. I pull on a sweater and, once out on the street, head for the home of a doctor friend of mine who lives ten blocks away. I walk along at a steady pace. The Park Avenue sidewalks are wide and almost empty. There are, however, some men who insist on helping me. They insist so much that I have to get angry. Everyone who is out tonight seems to be gay.

A man follows me; from his voice I can tell that he is well educated. He introduces himself as a professor from Boston whose immediate interest is the architecture of old New York houses. He complains that there is no respect for old things these days. Suddenly he exclaims:

'Oh, wait a minute! I'm going to describe something that will cheer you up. There's a young guy coming towards us in a wheelchair; he has no legs and he's being pushed by his male nurse. Doesn't that make you feel better?'

Flabbergasted, I hear the wheelchair go by as the professor shouts:

'Well, son! That's first-class transportation you have there!'

In a state of panic, I almost take to my heels. Having got rid of this refined gent by some gross insults, I hear another voice, charming but masculine:

'Walking alone?'

What a curious day it is when I frighten away the woman I love and attract only men.

The next morning, Désirée says:

'Oh, what a pretty sweater!'

Why does she say 'Oh, what a pretty sweater!' when she is familiar with my entire wardrobe? Suspicious, I inquire:

'What's pretty about it?'

'Why, it's pink.'

Among the things left behind by Valushka, there was a splendid baby-pink sweater. In my hurry to escape last night, I had put it on.

With a sweater of a more neutral colour, I feel reassured about my masculinity, which had been somewhat shaken by the events of the evening. Just as I am about to cross the street, a woman asks:

'Would you like me to help you?'

'No, thank you. It's all right.'

'You don't like women picking you up?'

Another woman stops me and asks:

'Don't you feel that the New York air is purer?'

It is true. The weather is fine and the sky is probably blue, but purer than what? She informs me:

'Purer since the Pope has been here.'

'Are you Catholic?'

'No, Presbyterian.'

In my wanderings, I have met all kinds of women. One evening as I was rushing to have dinner at the Café Carlyle, some policemen stopped me. I struggled and protested.

'Hold on, young man! Calm down! You almost knocked over the head of the British government.'

It was Mrs Thatcher, the iron lady!

And then there are the lunatics. The one who follows me for several blocks shouting 'Watch out! Watch out! Be careful!' And those who, perhaps deaf, know better than we do where we want to go. There is, for example, a woman whom I ask to help me cross 67th Street and who forces me, by pulling me along, to cross Park Avenue. When I feel the island in the middle of the avenue under my feet, I struggle and refuse to budge, as stubborn as a Moroccan donkey. She pulls, she pushes, and I absolutely refuse to move either backward or forward. She screams at me and goes off.

Since I have quickly become what the instructors call a 'good traveller' – that is, since I can move about in New York on my own – the rehabilitation centre asks me to help 'a client'. He is a black man, about thirty years old, who has become blind as a result of deterioration of the optic nerve. His greatest desire is to walk by himself in the street and his inability to do so is now his greatest frustration. He has been taking mobility classes for more than one year and still can't go out alone, even in his own neighbourhood. Full of self-doubt, he has fallen into a state of depression.

'I'm not good for anything. Don't waste your time. Something is wrong with my head.'

First of all, I talk to him. All he can express is his bitterness, and I soon come to agree with Jim – there is something wrong with his head. It's pride – 'When I walk down the street, I look ridiculous, grotesque' – and, more seriously, a lack of any spatial orientation. He is completely incapable of relating space to sound information. With an instructor, we go into a corridor and ask Jim to find the elevator. Eager to cooperate, he immediately sets off in the wrong direction, tapping the wall. Just then, at the other end of the corridor, the elevator arrives, the doors open and close, steps march off into the distance and fade away. During this time, Jim goes on tapping the wall. I stop him.

'Did you hear something?'

'Uh, yeah, somebody.'

'Did you hear a buzz?'

'Yes.'

'What do you think it was?'

'The elevator.'

'Then why are you still looking for it in front of you since the sound came from behind you?'

On top of that, Jim has been using this corridor and this elevator for more than a year. Some people think he is mentally deficient. No; I think he is simply panic-stricken. He's a good-looking black guy with his head full of macho clichés, and he cannot accept his new condition. If a woman offers to help him in the street, he doesn't answer or else he shouts back at her. If a man offers, he accepts more willingly.

'If coming from the Lighthouse you turn right, into Park Avenue, which street will you reach next?'

He can't give the answer. Yet it's a route he has taken, when accompanied, dozens of times. This guy is really in trouble. I suggest, to calm his pride, that he be given dancing lessons, that he learn how to move his body with grace and self-assurance. And then that he be introduced to spatial geometry, perhaps with a building game, using cubes, pyramids, spheres, etc.

I don't know how it will all turn out. But we do have one thing in common, and that's the desire to go out into the street by ourselves. The fact is that many blind people are not eager to do that. They are satisfied, as a survey has proved, with going only to those places they absolutely must. This same survey showed that at the end of a year, the number of miles covered is roughly the same whether the blind person is a 'good' or a 'bad' traveller. Very few go out alone simply for the pleasure of it.

Even though I am a 'good traveller', I know what it is to be completely flustered. Walking on Lexington once, I wanted to cross 57th Street, which goes in both directions. An animal fear gripped me and I couldn't cross. A primitive instinct of self-preservation prevented me from stepping into the street without seeing. Ashamed that my courage had disappeared, I set off anyway, and of course did so at the wrong time and in the worst way. I ran into cars and trucks and was saved in the nick of time by a passer-by, who screamed at me.

Confronted by what I was and what I am afraid of becoming, I am filled with rage. And it is these storms that sweep me up and hurl me against your door. I am tormented by not being able to take you away, to gallop off with you. This hateful impotence, this hellish fate that has soldered the visor of my helmet, which gave Samson the strength to tear down the temple. And it makes me violent enough to want to rape you, on the other's bed, thanking God for once that I cannot see your eyes.

'Go away, I hate you!' you told me.

And it was a relief to me. I thought that in this annihilation my pain would perish with your love. But no. I want even your hatred and you refuse it to me. And now, one day later, scraping the sidewalk with my cane, I feel like a cockroach. There are only your eyes, slightly sadder, slightly darker. They follow me down these corridors to the heart of the labyrinth, to the Minotaur, who sneers, 'The eye was in the tomb, watching.'

Too late. You are the one I was looking for, and I found you, but too late. A long time ago, when I was very young, I saw you. It was in a faraway province. I had left the road and walked through the woods until I reached the edge of a little valley. On the other slope, in blazing sunlight, stood a big house, and you were on the terrace. I watched you for a long time: you were wearing a white dress and in your hand you held an open book which you were not reading. There were flowers and espaliered fruit trees; everything radiated peace and happiness. Your hair was soaked with sunlight. I came back on the following days, but you didn't reappear and I swore to find you again. And now I know it is you. In losing you I lose not only the real but also the unreal, I lose the poetry. I saw you, very long ago and from too far away. I found you again too late; someone else had taken you and the beast had deprived me of light. You recognised me, but already they are all shouting, 'Make him go away!' You threw yourself into my arms and violence trembled all around us. But without light, how can I protect you, take you and carry you away? All I have to offer you is that inner light that you yourself radiate. You are the virgin pregnant with light, the virgin lucifer.

Too late – too late, let the fates decide.

TWENTY-FOUR

New Year's Day arrives as I wait for February 23. I have come with a few friends to spend the holiday at Pablo's, in Connecticut.

On this first morning of the year, I wake up early and go for a walk down the little road that passes in front of the house. It's the sort of morning that comes in the aftermath of a festivity – no cars, everybody is asleep, only dogs and birds; humans are all nursing hangovers. The earth is warm – it's as if the world were breathing out an immense thanksgiving to heaven. After walking for a mile or so, I come across a tiny brook flowing under the road, a brook which, like the birds and everything else, is singing. I sit down there, on the asphalt, above the trickle of water, to listen to it. And then, very soon, a dialogue is established. A prayer rises within me, a face-to-face with Life, what others would call God. I call upon the little brook to be the messenger to carry that prayer towards the sea, towards the World, towards the Beyond if there is one.

I stay there a long time, then I get up and continue walking. Completely lost in my thoughts, I move ahead by instinct. I hear something running towards me, but am too absorbed to pay attention to it. There is a shout; the animal in me rears up. I am afraid. I throw my hands and my cane in front of me to protect myself from a collision. Within me my heart has stopped. Everything stands still, frozen with fear. It is a jogger, wishing me 'Good morning.' He goes on, shouting 'Sorry!' over his shoulder.

I pause to catch my breath, to overcome the humiliation. Harmony shattered by so little.

A little farther on, just as I am getting over this shock, a small boy going by on a bicycle on the other side of the road says to me:

'Hello! Do you remember me? You came a long time ago to see my horse.'

'Oh, yes! How is he?'

'We sold him.'

'Why?'

In a hurt voice:

'He ate too much!'

'How sad that is! You must be very sad.'

'Oh, yes! I am very sad,' he says after thinking about it for a moment. I hear the bicycle moving away and his small voice saying 'Good-bye! Happy New Year!' So little and harmony is restored.

In Pablo's house everybody is up and he takes me to do some errands in Killingworth. After a few miles on the little country road, we run out of gas. No one around to help us.

'I'm going to push the car. All you have to do is hold the steering wheel.'

We begin to move. Behind the car, Pablo shouts his commands.

'. . . a sinistra. Adesso a destra, più a destra!'

He pushes. We begin to go faster; I even have the impression that we are moving fairly well when I hear the sound of a motorcycle arriving at the window and the voice of a policeman:

'Hello, sir. Do you need any help?'

I brake.

'It's all right. Everything is fine!'

But suddenly I realise that Pablo has taken advantage of a slight slope to get some rest, because I hear his laughter far behind. He runs up and declares:

'Anyway, officer, you can't give him a ticket! There may be a law against driving while drunk, but there isn't one against driving while blind.'

Coming back from that weekend in Connecticut, I go straight to the Lighthouse, without going home. Drained from a string of sleepless nights and bored by the repetition of the same routine, I had avoided going there for more than two weeks. Even though I don't apologise, Lesley seems happy to see me again. She takes me to Central Park.

I had insisted on her showing me a place I could get to alone from my apartment, where I might do some exercises or simply get some fresh air.

At 67th Street and Fifth, she asks me to find the entrance to the park. It's a small opening that I locate without any trouble because of the children's voices that pour from it and vanish into it. I notice this while Lesley is trying to describe the location of the entrance and how to reach it. I interrupt her and point my cane in the exact direction of the voices.

'It's there.'

She bursts out laughing.

'You don't need me.'

We follow an asphalt path into the park. Lesley explains that I must first find a tree and then locate in relation to it a plot of grass where I can do my gymnastics.

I stop and listen. I seem to hear a tree just ahead of me, on the left. I listen very attentively; I am not really sure whether I actually do hear something; I am not yet sure of my interpretations. So I move ahead in what I assume to be the right direction and listen again. And there, very distinctly, I hear it, I sense it. I am approaching it, or at least I think I am. It's a presence more than a direction. I take some steps forward and sense it more acutely. I swing my cane through space. It isn't there. I take another step. Nothing. A step to the left. Nothing. I wave my cane to the right. Still nothing! I stop. . . . I hear it. Exasperated, I throw my cane down on the ground.

'That's too much! I hear that tree but can't locate it!'

She cracks up.

'You brushed against it three times, or, rather, missed it three times by a hair!'

My hearing seems to have become more acute. I hear objects, obstacles, from a greater distance. It is a skill I have developed very quickly.

On the way back, I sense that Lesley is in rather low spirits.

We have been working together on a daily basis for a little more than a year. She tells me she missed me during my two-week absence. I am embarrassed.

'Let's go have a cup of coffee. I know a coffee shop near here.'

She agrees, but I sense in her voice that she would like to have coffee at my place. We go to the coffee shop anyway, since I'm out of coffee. Once there, she tells me:

'I feel depressed. I've been at the Lighthouse for three years and the work isn't always that much fun.'

'Maybe it's time for you to leave. It's a rough place. You give a great deal but you don't get much in return. A lot of the clients take you for granted. You're still young. Leave!'

She did leave. I was practically her last client.

The thought of this coming operation obsesses me. The anxiety created by Dr T.'s words has not dissolved. 'You're taking an unnecessary risk.' How can I be sure?

Several times in my life, with a healthy scepticism, I have consulted fortunetellers: in Africa, the priests of Fa; in Asia, the geomancers of *I Ching*; in Harlem, Dwike. This time, I go to see a cabalistic divinator. He lives in this old decaying palace on New York's upper West Side, at the Ansonia. We have an appointment at three o'clock in the afternoon. I am waiting in front of the elevator for someone to go up so that I can locate the third-floor button. Finally, a little old lady comes, and I ask her to push the button. As she rummages in her bag, I grow impatient and repeat my request.

'Just a minute, young man. I'm looking for my magnifying glass so I can read the number.'

I wander around on that vast third floor until a cleaning woman shows me to door number 30A. I ring, the floor creaks, and the door opens a crack. I give my name. Silence. Then a wheezing voice tells me hurriedly:

'I can't do anything for you. I can't do anything, and, in any case, you'd have to be able to write.'

But when I've come all the way across Manhattan and have had to conquer unfamiliar corridors, no one is going to close the door in my face so easily. I put my foot in the door. A hand pushes me back but I feel as static as a rock.

'I write perfectly well, and you'll see that everything will be all right.'

The door opens, I go in, he closes it and moves farther into the stale air of the apartment. He makes me sit down opposite him, at a little bridge table.

'Write down your questions and give me a familiar object.'

I write the words *operation* and *book* on two pieces of paper, which I fold up carefully.

He grasps the bits of paper in one hand and with the other takes my watch, which I hold out to him. Then, in a hoarser voice, with the words rushing out, he recites:

'Our Father Mother God
In heaven and on earth
We ask thy blessing upon us
As we sit together
We pray for guidance
We pray for wisdom we pray for understanding.

'Help us to solve our life
In such a way as to fulfil
The karma of this incarnation
In so doing achieve the greatest happiness
Health peace and security
But most especially to find
Continued and greater opportunity
Of service to our fellow beings
And thus to be of service to thee.
Amen.'

He concentrates.

'I see your aura, which is the atmosphere that your thoughts and feelings create around you. This electromagnetic field is the very expression of our energy. Yours is limpid, with clearly defined edges, not at all blurred. And that is remarkable, considering that you have just become blind and must have been caught up in a terrible storm. Still, I don't see any storm around you. In fact, over your head I can see a golden flame, as bright as a candle, and that is creativity.

> '*I see: fire in your brain*
> *fire in your hands*
> *fire in your heart*
> *fire in your sex*
> *fire in your feet*

'The fire in your head is intelligence. The fire in your hands is creativity. The combination head-heart-hands should produce something in the realm of Mercury. Mercury is Hermes, the messenger of the gods. It is either something written or something which will come out of your hands. At any rate, it is something you will give birth to, a child of your brain, something that is already on the way. In any case, the next ten years will be the most productive of your life.

'But I see you in a hospital, I see you getting your sight back. You may think that's impossible but it's exactly what I see, and I hope I am not mistaken. I don't know whether it will be for surgery or something else, but I know you will be hospitalised. I know that you will be in intensive care, that it will take a long time and that it will seem endless to you.

'You are discouraged, but only on the surface. Deep down, you are afraid and, beneath it all, there is a conflict among three things: determination, hope, and fear. Such a conflict is human.

'In spite of, not because of, your blindness, you will succeed, spurred by that determination you have within you. But because you are human, you will experience discouragement. Up to now, you have been managing very well. If I were you, I wouldn't bother with Braille and the other nonsense. For me, it would even be an act of faith. You must accept your condition, accept even the possibility of its becoming permanent. You say to yourself, "OK! I accept this goddam cane and, now and then, a little help from other people, but I'd rather hang than become one of those helpless blind men you find begging on street corners. I am certainly not going to let others pity me." In any case, they are going to pity you. They mean well, but, as you know, they're more of an insult than anything else. You will see again. Is it physically possible according to the doctors?'

'Yes.'

'Hospitalisation, sight. 1980 will be the year for both.'

'I already have an appointment.'

'You must go through with it. I see an operation. But as for the rest, I don't see anything. You will come out of it richer but you will have gone through hell.

'You don't sit around feeling sorry for yourself. I see move-ment, a change of residence; you may or may not want it, but it's going to happen; you are going to begin travelling again. There is fire in your feet, like the gypsies.

'. . . I don't understand. Are you a writer? Is that your profession? I see a publication. It will be successful.'

He unfolds the two little pieces of paper.

'Operation, oh, sure! As for the book, it is written, or else you are writing it now. You will die far, far away from the place you were born. You will travel widely, you will take long trips, especially from 1980 on. For the time being, you are stuck. Stay stuck. Well, there you are, that's all.'

'How much do I owe you?'

'Nothing at all; there's no fee. You will pay the next time, when you'll be able to see me.'

The door closes behind me. See, I will see again! Already I am walking down the corridor as if I could see. I am only temporarily blind. I reach the sidewalk with a confidence that surprises me. The sun shines on Manhattan. My heart is bursting. Once again, everything is possible. I will emerge from the black labyrinth and the Minotaur will be defeated.

My black taxi driver is singing to himself, and at the end of the ride categorically refuses to let me pay him.

I will see again, and today everything is free.

I will see again. I work out the dates – February 23, first operation; end of May, all will be over. In July, I will leave for the Island, to 'see' Valushka. To come upon her gently in the raw light that cleans wounds deep to the bone frightens me. The revelation of her soul on her face, in her eyes, must not be seen under too harsh a light. I want to look at her as sailors look in wonder at a galleon laden with gold that surges from the abyss, moved by some mysterious phenomenon.

I will leave, and already I burn my bridges, distributing my belongings, returning things people had lent me, entrusting my piano to a little girl with nimble fingers, sadly abandoning Valushka's tree. In three days I am to leave for Mexico to work on my body, making it strong and supple before submitting to Dr A.'s scalpel. In three days . . . and the Crime Victims Compensation Board has still not decided whether to grant me the money needed for the operation. In the apartment, which is now full of echoes, the telephone rings. It is Marilyn, the young woman at the bank who takes care of my simple account. She informs me of a thirteen-thousand-dollar cheque with Valushka's signature on it and asks me what she should do with it. I hang up quickly, call Valushka, thank her, and turn down her offer.

'I'm sure that the Crime Victims Board will give me the money, and anyway the operation costs twelve thousand, not . . .'

'Don't be silly. Don't waste your time on such details, and I prefer thirteen because it brings luck.'

Thirteen thousand dollars is what her grandmother left her when she died.

I learn that February 23 falls on a Saturday. Suspecting some mistake, I phone Dr A. in Barcelona.

'Excuse me, Doctor, did you know that February 23 is a Saturday? Can you confirm that date?'

'I'm not the one who continually changes the date of this operation! When I say February 23, I mean February 23. So are you coming or not?'

'I'm coming, I'm coming! It's only because . . .'

'Excuse me, I don't have any time now.'

And he hangs up.

TWENTY-FIVE

In three weeks, Barcelona. For this land of hope I must strengthen my body. In that arena of the operating room, hope will either disappear or emerge victorious. Whatever the outcome, the shock will be tremendous: I will either see again or be blind forever. One must be fully armed, and for that reason I am leaving for the Pacific coast of Mexico.

A villa on the summit of a mountain overlooking the sea and, dominating everything, an immense concrete cross. The slopes of this Golgotha are dripping with millionaires' villas surrounded by walls and armed guards. Children try to sneak in from downtown to eat from the garbage cans. I wonder what they think of the enormous crucifix towering over them.

The heat, the humidity, the smells, the wind from the sea, the stink of exhaust fumes spat out by broken-down engines; all this takes me back to Bangkok, Medan, Cotonou, Denpasar, Saigon. To know that any kind of adventure is impossible, that no chance meeting will occur, that I will not be able to sit in a bar to observe people in everyday life makes me break down. Sitting next to my unopened bag, I stupidly begin to cry. Outside the window, beyond the flowers and the scents, lies the most beautiful bay in the world, indifferent and, to me, absent.

My host brings me a Scotch and asks:

'What do you miss the most since losing your eyesight?' I answer immediately:

'Adventure.'

'What do you mean?'

'Life which, through conquest, leads you to knowledge. I feel as if I've been thrown to the ground.'

'On the road to Damascus?'

'No, I didn't hear any voice.'

As far as adventure is concerned, I already know that I'll leave here without having met with it. I am shut up in this villa, with its luxurious garden and swimming pool, and I have no way of escaping, no way at all.

Later, at the open-air market in the old city, I stand still, taking in the smells of spices, flowers, sweaty bodies; listening to the whimpering of children; examining the baskets. This life lived close to the earth and all these sun-drenched fruits make me high. I feel like an escaped prisoner.

In the villa up on the hill I set to work. Three hours a day, I swim up and down the pool, and let the sun do its work. After a week, sunburned and aching all over, I already feel much better. My body has expanded and I would like space to expand, too, but the swimming pool, a thousand times swum, seems to have shrunk.

And there is the Playa Encantada, the Enchanted Beach, which is deserted except for a cabin with an old policeman. He has wrapped his pistol in plastic 'so it won't rust.' During the daytime, he stops the cows from grazing on a bed of sickly flowers and at night he keeps robbers from stealing tiles off the roof. In front of us, the immense Pacific, and at the end of the beach, Patagonia. Thousands of miles of sand, I am drunk with space. I jump, do cartwheels, and try for the first time to run without a guide. It is against nature to run without sight. Even though I know that there are no obstacles between me and Patagonia, I must learn to dismiss my obsessive concern with walls, trees, rocks, and holes.

I plunge into the water, which extends to the China Sea. Breakers crash against me. First one, then two, then three, and I dive into the wave. Refreshed, I want to stand up. The ground has disappeared. This is so unexpected that it gives me a shock and I am panic-stricken. I begin to swim towards the beach, but can't get my footing. I remain motionless, aware that my whole body is being tugged at by a current. I realise that I am being carried along by an undertow. I swim harder and, suddenly, am hit by a wave full in the face. Then I realise that I am moving farther towards the open sea. The fear of sharks increases my panic, and I start to lose the rhythm of my breathing. If I don't get hold of myself, I am dead. The waves are so loud and the beach so wide that there is no point in shouting. In any case, I will find out later that the man who has come with me doesn't know how to swim. It is about two o'clock. Through my eyelids, I get my bearings in relation to the sun, deduce the position of the beach, and keep going in that direction without allowing myself the time to doubt. I swim and swim, it's a question of faith. Finally, exhausted, I reach the shore.

Completely out of breath, I stagger along the beach, not knowing which way to go. Because of the current I have drifted below the cabin. As I walk, I clap my hands and call for help. A moment later, my companion's voice warns me:

'Watch out for currents and sharks! The old man says this beach is dangerous.'

It's about time! The dull roar of the ocean, which had initially sounded out a message of freedom on this enchanted beach, is now full of menace.

The night is hot and the crickets are singing, and I wonder how I will fare with this operation. Maybe with a black patch over one eye, and the other with a fixed stare.

Tonight I feel like laughing, having a good time, because I feel so tense. Will I come out of it a monster? And what will I do with this sight, which will probably be very limited?

Tonight I drink. I start off with a Scotch at the home of Madame D., who has invited us to dinner. Almost as soon as I arrive, she takes me aside.

'I must talk to you.' And she has me sit down on her right.

Musicians immediately surround us. She barks at them:

'Go play somewhere else. You're breaking my eardrums!'

I can just feel revolvers rattling in their holsters. She murmurs:

'You know, I spent seven months in a concentration camp in Cuba.'

Why the devil does she tell me that? An excuse? Champagne,

violins, laughter, fireworks – clearly, she is trying to forget.

She introduces me to the French ambassador, then excuses herself, leaving me alone with him. A few seconds go by, and I hear his footsteps moving away without his having said a word to me. What diplomacy! Obviously, he wasn't prepared for this kind of conversation. Nobody has taught him his lines.

Later, a woman comes and sits down beside me. She speaks a funny kind of French, claims to be part French herself, and the conversation takes this surrealistic turn:

'Vous habitez français? Do you know someone whose name is Baron de Rothschild?'

'I've heard of him.'

'Mon Dieu! What a small world! Just think, he's a good friend of mine.'

'It's the world of money, madam, which is small.'

Two nights later, another dinner is given for Olivia Newton-John, a singer whose name means nothing to me. Water serves as the dining-room floor. The table, a huge slab of steel, is suspended from the ceiling by chains; the chairs are on a raft. The waiters have a hell of a time balancing themselves, let alone the dishes.

Next to me is a young man who is studying in New York. I don't recognise the name of the college he attends.

'Actually, I live in New York but I go to school in Connecticut. I rent a plane three times a week to get there.'

'I hope you are getting good grades!'

He doesn't understand my concern.

After these two dinners, I am ill-at-ease. But that makes little difference. Mexico has given me what I had come to find. I feel light-hearted as I climb aboard the plane.

TWENTY-SIX

Saturday, February 23. I have not been admitted into the Barraquer Clinic. I phoned yesterday, but my name was not on the admission list. Somewhat astonished, I asked to speak to Dr A. The voice on which I count so desperately, which can raise or dash my hopes with every inflection, answers:

'But what do you think? That I work on weekends?'

'Not at all, Doctor, and that's why I phoned you from New York.'

'You phoned to cancel the operation. I don't have time to waste with these details, just talk to my secretary. Come in on Monday morning at ten o'clock and I will examine you.'

'Should I bring my pyjamas?'

'I have told you that you should consult my secretary for details.'

This tension between Dr A. and me continues. I don't understand why he is so brutal. And yet he must be perfectly aware of the tightrope of hope on which I am perched and how precarious my balance is. What disturbs me the most is that I know from other sources not only that he is the best in the world for this kind of case, but also that he is a kind man. For the poorer patients he operates for nothing. So what is it about me that has aroused such hostility? I wonder if I am not simply a victim of the Spanish Civil War, if the important lady whose family is well known for supporting Franco has not been pushing my case to him without my knowing. Dr A. is not pro-Franco; from what I have been able to find out about him, he comes from a part of Spain that is leftist and that suffered a great deal from Franco's victory. Perhaps he automatically associates me with the political class of a lady who has recommended me. What a terrible, pointless misunderstanding! In the war I am waging, this particular battle seems like a tragic waste of energy. I am neither a fascist nor rich.

The tightrope I am on is so taut that I am able to feel and interpret every vibration. Undergoing my operation on Valushka's birthday seemed to me, as far as the stars are concerned, an ideal coincidence. And then there was an incident which startled and upset me so much that I still try to banish it from my thoughts. Arriving at the Hotel Colón, I pay for the taxi, put my money in my pocket, and take the arm of the doorman, who has picked up my bags. Just then, something brutal and aggressive rams into my jacket pocket, like a wild boar's snout digging into the ground. My hand seizes another hand, which continues to rummage. I stammer, not knowing how to shout 'Stop! Thief!' in Spanish. The doorman, who is on the other side of me and doesn't see or understand anything, answers:

'Sí, sí, la puerta, aquí mismo.'

I grab the man's wrist, but he breaks away with far more strength than is necessary. The suddenness, violence, and cynicism of this act leave a nightmarish fog in my head, and stir up memories of the night in MacDougal Alley. I must stop them immediately. The hotel employees are all excited now, shouting, commenting, running in the street, eager to discuss the incident with me at length. I tell them:

'The money is gone, and so is the thief. There's nothing we can do, so let's drop the subject.'

The fear I had felt in that man was as dangerous as a knife.

My room is at the end of a complicated network of corridors. It is small, not very clean, and looks out over a courtyard. No sounds from outside can be heard. The night passes in silence and solitude. I toss and turn, obsessed with hope. My brain short-circuits from listening to its own thoughts. It is 3:00 A.M. I must, I absolutely must, talk to Valushka, but she has changed her telephone number so that I won't be tempted to call. I know the name of one of her relatives in Paris; information quickly gives me the Paris number. I assume the authoritative voice of an Arab businessman who can't be bothered with polite formalities. The poor woman, awakened in the middle of the night, is only too happy to look up the number, just to be rid of me. I try to call New York, but the operator must have gone to sleep, because the line is dead.

In the dusty recesses of this cubicle, my last connection with the outside world has just been cut off. Regardless of how much I toy with the phone, it remains dead. Under no circumstances will I stay in this isolated hole. I must go and rouse the sleeping desk clerk. I wander down the corridors, feeling my way along mouldings, doors; there are no windows. I hear hallways opening up sometimes to the right, sometimes to the left, and I pass through a glass door that squeaks abominably. I locate an up staircase but can't find the corresponding one that should go down. I try to keep my bearings; I will need to be able to find my way back. Suddenly I hear a rumbling interrupted by suppressed sighs – the elevator. A late-returning guest says, 'Buenas noches.' I hold the door and hurl myself inside, randomly pushing several of the lower buttons, half expecting to set off an alarm bell. But miraculously the elevator jerks to a halt in the lobby. The desk clerk grudgingly reconnects my line. It has taken me almost an hour of navigating between Scylla and Charybdis to reach him, but I prefer not to mention it.

I find my way back to my room fairly easily, but nevertheless I turn the handle slowly, open the door a crack, and listen for breathing; after all, all the doors are identical in this hotel, and I could easily have made a mistake. I dial Valushka's number. On the other side of the Atlantic, the phone rings five times, ten times, fifteen times. She is not at home.

Time stands still, and in the silence I touch the hands of my watch, which seem to be soldered to the dial. 'I will examine you.' What more does he want to examine? Perhaps he no longer wants to reopen my eyes or attempt a major operation. The only thing I want is to lie down on his table and have him operate on me. I am certain that if we reach that point, his genius and my faith will restore the visible world to me. To get onto that table, I'll do practically anything. Neither his rough treatment nor his rebuffs will stop me; somehow I'll get around them.

Very early in the morning I hear the cathedral bells in the distance over the rooftops. It is Sunday and Spain is asleep. The ringing of the telephone and Valushka's underwater voice shatter my solitude:

'He didn't operate on you!'

I explain. She calms me down:

'That makes no difference. I trust him. Don't be silly; he's an extraordinary man. He's going to operate on you. Don't stay alone. Phone Antonio.'

And silence closes up again like a cocoon around her voice, which goes on singing in my head all day. In this tightrope crossing she is the balancing pole. I don't feel like seeing anyone; nevertheless, I call Antonio, who is indignant with me for not having come to stay with him, and he invites me to dinner. He is a pianist, which I didn't know, and he plays the Goldberg Variations magnificently.

The next morning, he accompanies me to the clinic, and I am quite surprised when the receptionist concedes that I do indeed have an appointment with Dr A. at ten o'clock. The crowd is there with its smell of sweat and black tobacco and the children bumping into my legs and holding onto my pants. Antonio has to leave, but I have little time left to wait.

I am shown into Dr A.'s office and this time, since I know my way around, I manage to avoid any disturbing handling by the nurse. I put my head back into the cold apparatus; Dr A.'s voice is cordial, and he says nothing about my glasses or about our misunderstanding over the date. Then he sets out once again to test my sense of projection with the little penlight: 'Where is it now? . . . And now? . . . Where? . . . Now where is it? . . . How about now? . . . And now?' Once again I lie. Totally diffused in my head, the light seems to come from all directions. The important thing is to get myself onto that damned operating table.

He returns to his desk and remains silent for a long time.

'You perceive the light well, but you don't really know if it's coming from above or below, left or right. I must open you up, that's the first step, before trying the odonto-keratoprosthesis. Tomorrow I'll open the eyelids, just the eyelids, you understand. Don't eat anything for at least twelve hours beforehand. There is atrophy; if, in addition, your projection is not good, nothing can be done. I want that to be quite clear. OK? Any questions?'

'Yes. If the results of this operation are positive, when would you perform the major operation?'

'We'll know in two days, but I doubt if it will come to that, because I think the outcome of the first investigation will be negative. You must be very, very sure that this is quite clear to you.'

'Yes, yes, I understand. But let's just suppose there's a miracle.'

'A miracle? OK. Then you will go into the clinic the following week for the first phase. All right? To avoid any haemorrhaging, buy these shots at the pharmacy – I'm writing it down for you – and have somebody give you one tonight and one tomorrow morning when you check in for the operation. I want you to understand very, very well that we are simply *opening* the eyelids so that later on you won't say that I told you something different. See you tomorrow morning, at nine. Mademoiselle, call the person who is accompanying Monsieur de Montalembert.'

'I am by myself.'

'How's that? You can't go through this alone. You should have friends, some family with you!'

I hear him muttering:

'Really! Unheard of!'

They draw a blood sample, listen to my heart, take my blood pressure, and test my reflexes, all of which proves to me, if any proof is needed, that the operation is imminent. The stethoscope presses against my skin, still tanned from the Mexican sun. As always, the approaching action clears my head. I detest waiting, monotony, and routine. And yet it is with those very ingredients that empires have been built. I am not an empire builder; I love living and I love communicating this appetite for life.

Tonight I feel like shouting out my joy in being alive, I feel like laughing with all the staff at the Barraquer Clinic; in my soul, I am singing of you, Valushka, you who started me out on this path of light, who, out of love, are thrusting me onto the operating table. I shout to you so that, in spite of all the disconnected telephones, you will hear me.

Outside, on the steps where the Swede was stabbed a few months earlier, the air is gentle and smells of the sweetness of an impatient spring. The jasmines have burst into bloom. The Mediterranean Sea, there at the end of the street, rests, waiting for the rape of the summer. If all goes well, I will see again, see the summer, the sea, and, for the first time, Valushka.

Taxi! I am going to Antonio's, where there is a party. I am already drunk, drunk with impatience and hope. Piano, gypsy guitar music. A young girl they call La Panthera slaps the floor with the soles of her feet. Tequila blooms within me. Aie! . . . let the party go on, for I cannot sleep. Aie! . . . the sound of Paco de Lucia's guitar! And that Catalonian wine, so heavy that, when it spills, you can pick it up and throw it away. Aie! . . . what is this pain? It is your dark eyes that keep staring at me. Let me get drunk on music and alcohol, for I am suffocating with joy. 'That's not a very good way to prepare for an operation,' you tell me, in that prim way of yours. 'See how strong I am, I can pass right through the wall!'

The following morning I have to shake Antonio awake so that he can drive me to the clinic, because I'm not familiar with the neighbourhood and don't know where the taxis are.

They assign me a room, and I climb immediately into bed wearing the pyjamas I've bought especially for the occasion. In this foreign outfit, which smells of starch and scratches my skin, I wait, feeling a bit ridiculous about lounging in bed without being either tired or sick. A nurse gives me the last injection of coagulant. Antonio has left with an apology: his mother has to undergo a gallbladder operation this same morning.

On the bedside table, there is a telephone. If only I could hear that singing voice! I wait here until a quarter to twelve. Suddenly, there is a rush of footsteps. 'Come! The doctor is ready for the operation. Come!'

I had thought it would be the same as in New York and that I would be wheeled into the operating room. At least there will be no slippers. I detest slippers as much as pyjamas, so in my tennis shoes I proceed down the hall. I am rushed along, for it seems that the doctor is running late. We walk to an elevator, which takes us down one floor, walk down yet more hallways, take another elevator, and continue until we reach one of the bottom floors. We follow a series of catacomblike tunnels. I have the distinct impression of having reached the heart of the labyrinth, where the blind beast lies, now anaesthetised. The walls get closer together and the doors are finally so low that I have to bend over to avoid bumping my forehead. At last we reach what seems to be a closet. The clatter of dishes, steel instruments striking against enamel basins, all those kitchen sounds of an operating room. Hands fit me with a gown, stretch me out on the operating table, and strap me down. A cap is put on my head. The anaesthesiologist takes hold of my right arm and says to me as he inserts the needle:

'You're going to get a whiff of Neapolitan pizza.'

Sure enough, the taste of garlic fills my mouth. I am indeed on the edge of the Mediterranean, where even anaesthesia has the flavour of the local cuisine.

Here I am. I have just woken up and am trying to talk into my tape recorder. But the bandage, like an octopus, paralyses my face. It is about two o'clock. In my mouth garlic has turned into benzine. I have a headache but my brain is at least functioning. There is a tight feeling around my eyes. Cautiously, I lift up a piece of tape, relaxing the pressure on my upper lip. And I wait, wait impatiently, to see Dr A. and to learn the outcome of his investigation. Automatically, I feel my teeth, although I know they weren't to be involved this time. I'm hungry, I'm thirsty, and I want a cigarette. Gradually the effect of the anaesthesia wears off and the pain starts to become 'ultraviolet', as Valushka would say. At long last, a nurse consents to bring me a cup of coffee and a madeleine. She informs me that Dr A. won't come by until tomorrow morning. What a disappointment! Why must I wait until tomorrow morning? Valushka has not telephoned.

How strange my life is: they open my eyes while I'm asleep and shut them again when I wake up.

It is ten o'clock at night. Dr A. has just left. I don't have to wait until tomorrow. He tells me:

'You must stay calm, Monsieur de Montalembert. You must not get excited.'

And my heart jumps, for joy, for what could possibly get me excited if not hope, the possibility of a different kind of future? The operation will be performed. I am going to see again, dimly, no doubt, but it will certainly no longer be this blackness. There will not be this wall between you and me, this thing that my gaze cannot penetrate. I am going to be able to direct my eyes, or at least one eye, far off into the distance, free myself from this claustrophobia, escape from the dark labyrinth, and slit the Minotaur's throat.

'You must stay calm. I opened up your eyelids, and nothing can be done.'

I miss the rest of what he says: 'opened . . . eyelids . . . atrophy . . . projection . . . very bad.' No hope, there is absolutely no hope. I will die blind. I refuse to let myself cry for fear that tears so soon after the operation will burn my eyes. I am ice cold. I extend my hand, which he takes.

'Thank you, Doctor, for having tried, and also for having always been honest with me. You have always said you thought nothing could be done.'

'I will stay in touch with you.'

He picks up my mini-tape recorder.

'Ten years ago, no one knew that such instruments would be made. Nowadays, with cybernetics and other such sciences, researchers are making discoveries every day. Perhaps, in ten or twenty years, I will be able to try something. If you were eighty, I would tell you that it's not impossible but that you must wait, and you would die without having lost hope. But you are young, and it's better for you to look at life the way it is. But don't remain alone!'

His voice is incredibly gentle, and I sense that he is overcome with pity. I feel a desperate need to talk to Valushka and, at the same time, I'm afraid to. She has fought so hard for her hope. She has wanted so passionately for me to see again. I don't know how to break the news to her. I feel very tired. I have fought, and fought alone, which is the way such a battle should be waged. I have fought well, and in the end I have been defeated.

So many questions come up. What is my life going to be like during the forty or fifty years to come? I feel calm, but I hear the slow sadness of my beating heart. I do not hold this against God, or life, or myself.

An Italian-speaking nurse puts a sleeping pill on my table. I don't know whether I'll use it, but I won't hesitate to do so if it seems necessary.

Silence. I am alone in this room. No one calls. The telephone doesn't ring. It's better that way. I'm afraid that people will be afraid. Some of them were so optimistic. They would even tell me which eye was going to see again. Fortunately, I always took that certainty for what it was: their intense desire to wish me well. I know that I can break down today, tonight, tomorrow, or later. I could very easily break down. I'm not sure of myself. The situation is horrible enough for me to be well aware of the danger. I will get my strength back, but for the moment I feel defeated. I think of Valushka, of the Island. I would have loved to have that improbable meeting and to see her suddenly one night by a temple in the glowing light of oil lamps, then, as if to soften this first vision of her, with our eyes meeting as best they can.

It can't be denied that I have lost the battle, physically. I wonder about the clotted life that lies ahead. Through the window comes the slow music of a fountain on the patio, like a life trickling away and disappearing. There is nothing emptier than a burned-out head. Out of this devastation, out of these ashes, no flower can ever bloom again. Aho, what is to become of me? There he is, looking at me, but with a look so far, so far beyond me. There is in his eyes that melancholic mist, that meditative air, which always gives me a certain vertigo.

'Men often think that their individual fate is everything. They are tools. It is enough to contemplate Mahù, the Creator himself, for he is greater than fate. He is the Man-of-the-World, Mahù Logpé Yewé. He alone sets limits to the knowledge that man is allowed to acquire about himself and his fate. Your eyes are rascals: they left for the world of the dead without waiting for you. Eyes are for perceiving danger; they have departed before your death, so danger will no longer come from the visible world.'

'But, Aho, they also let me perceive beauty!'

'Beauty is a shadow that is borne by every object, every person, like the signature of the Creator, just as I taught you. Your fingers are already touching the heart of things. You will see those things that light makes invisible. You will see the little shadow in the shadow. You will see beauty, the signature. Listen to that fountain. Don't you see every tiny drop of it?'

It's true. I see and scrutinise every drop like the sparkling of diamonds.

I took the sleeping pill and this morning I woke up with these words hammering in my head: 'No hope, no hope.' Life is a tremendous anvil on which you can be either forged or broken. The bandage across my eyes has loosened and the pain is now bearable. How ashamed I feel, even though I don't know just why. Should I leave for the Island and confront Valushka with this reality? What am I to do? Leave New York and go to Paris? My intellectual life would perhaps be easier there; in any case, my physical life seems permanently compromised.

I phoned Valushka to tell her that I will never see her. She didn't say a word. There was a long silence. I could hear her breathing so close. I said good-bye and hung up. I will leave the Barraquer Clinic. I feel as empty as a woman who has undergone an abortion.

TWENTY-SEVEN

Thirty-six thousand Tartars come galloping down and trample upon my soul tonight. Thirty-six thousand Tartars, drunk with rape, are devastating you in me tonight. Thirty-six thousand Tartars have taken their sabres and split the space that united us. The madness has been extinguished and the established order has reasserted its rights and its rituals. And I remain on this black sand and my soul is loath to love you. I would like simply to place the tips of my fingers upon you. I understand that my ravished light is an object of horror. I feel exiled from your beauty and above all from your light. What overwhelms me is that you have made me lose myself in love. Now I am so close to you that I am cold when I am near others, and this wound in my side is a menace to them. I wake up at night, covered with sweat that, in my dream, I thought was yours. I am in a solitude that is yours, in the company of your absence. Sometimes the wind brings me the scent of your sex and I dream of pale flowers that I penetrate. Defeated, you fled, leaving me unconscious. It had to be: your eyes were already becoming listless, for my fate is a kind of leprosy. Curiously, you were the one who was more defeated in Barcelona when the doctor told me, 'Nothing can be done.' I didn't know how to face up to your sorrow, how to announce to you that my leprosy was permanent. I listened to your soul and I heard it murmur, 'I want to live, live, live.'

Why have I come back to this island, when the wind that rises every evening gives me the signal for a departure that is no longer possible? The crash of waves at night now frightens me, for the damage is serious and I risk sinking into the deep. On the shore of this tropical sea I feel like one of those gutted hulls, of which so many can be found in the ports around here. Their shape is still beautiful and you would think it's enough to hoist the sails and race along, cutting the waves in a perfect trajectory. Don't you see that gaping hole under the water line? The line of the ship is so beautiful and the sea is so free that no one wants to see the splintered timbers. The passer-by says, looking at the boat, 'It is quite reparable.' He doesn't even notice that man sitting there on the sand, the ship's captain, shrugging his shoulders.

How many people have told me, 'It's reparable. You'll see. I can't tell you why, but I know it.' A woman who works at the Lighthouse, an intelligent and sensible woman, told me confidentially, 'Listen! I don't know how to tell you this. I'm used to the blind, but with you I feel something different. You will see again, at least with one eye.' It's reparable, everyone agrees, it's quite reparable. Everyone but the doctors and the captain.

With Valushka, it's different, because she wasn't content just to look at the hull and say that one day it would float again. She flung me on the operating table to have the damage repaired. After the verdict, knowing that she could never set sail and become intoxicated with the freedom that even in my wrecked state I still bear witness to, she moved sadly away. The unbearable absence of her look saved me from being stranded in the sand. I hoisted sail and, with water leaking in on all sides, I took off for those shores that I had described to her and where I knew she would go. I reached them but was terrified. Several times, I thought I was going to sink into the deep, spending nights bailing out anguish as it rose through the opening in the bottom of the hold. And when, at last, I rejoined her, I looked even more, on the shore of my former freedom, like a pathetic wreck. I recognised this clearly in her voice, which suddenly backed away, and I was too proud to accept it. I have not seen her again and she has not looked for me.

The rooms of this empty hotel reek of mould. I take the pulse of night and gulp the terror of the silence. I feel imprisoned within my skin. I no longer know anything and am in the limbo that precedes birth or death. At the bottom of this well, desire vanishes; time stretches endlessly and nothing moves. I no longer listen, no longer wait. In the seventh tower of silence, I dance towards the sun. In the eighth tower of silence, I shake off my ashes. Embers from the moon flow through my veins. Stone by stone, walls rise up around me; stone by stone, they become impenetrably thick. Void, anguish, emptiness like a single heavy beam in the sea. I should cry out, but how can I force the moon to be the sun? At this point, blackness has almost become a friendly presence. I surrender to darkness, which triumphs. I have lost light's secret and innocence withdraws when faced by this desert which frightens me. I stop resisting and drown in these stifling shadows. I have no more thoughts; I am lost in a dream of silence. Escape, escape . . . will I ever escape? On the other side of the wall, the sea is carrying off a grain of sand forever lost to me. Everything is moving away, except the walls. It is life itself that is committing my suicide! I talk to myself and I hear an enemy's voice. Seven years ago, I was full of confidence, but, today, how can I believe? A black beast is sitting on my shoulder and forces me to yield. Where has my solitude fled? Or is it you who robbed me of it? I tumble down to the ocean's floor – what agony! And the monsters of the deep come rushing at me. I am tired and would like to lie down on the curve of the horizon.

Seven years ago, I came to the Island, after the horror of Vietnam. I had been told that here one's belief in the beauty of the world could be restored, and it was true. Having come for a month, I stayed a year. I saw everything: the volcanoes, the flowers, the dances, the rivers, the temples. I explored where there were no roads, where people said there was nothing to be seen, which meant, in fact, that reality was more brutal there. I sailed in wooden skiffs with fishermen in search of turtles towards islands where no one wants to land. That was seven years ago.

With this visit, I feel as if I have recovered a part of myself that had been left behind. I have walked around the Island, stumbling over the tombs of my own life. People, music, smells,

Agung the little dancer, who is now married, children's voices, the sounds of the sea – they are like tombs that I bump into, that I try to open. The first nights I wanted to flee, to fly off at dawn, to catch the first plane in the morning, to go back to my own kind and my own culture, to take shelter behind the walls of my childhood. Every night I want to run away from the very present absence of Valushka, who is somewhere on the Island. But day breaks, and the singing birds dissolve my black insomnia.

'Salamat Pagi! Do you recognise me?'

It is Parwata, who came here with me seven years ago on the Bugis boat and with whom I was twice shipwrecked. Parwata, as handsome as Arjuna, with a black lion's mane framing his imperiously proud face. Parwata, who with one look could make faint the hearts of the *juanitas* of Alas and Sumbawa Besar, whose piercing eyes would shred the violet veils of the Muslim girls of Solo. A champion of the martial arts, his twenty-two-year-old body covered with knife scars, he was ready for any kind of adventure, any kind of deal, as long as there were danger and money involved. Seven years ago, Parwata refused to accept the mediocrity that his companions were content with. Pride and courage flamed within him.

Seven years later, his voice is thicker, his body heavier. He works at the hotel reception desk, taking orders from a Chinese. He is married and has three children; but I sense from the way he talks that it was his wife who married him. She has a beauty parlour in Denpasar. 'Oh, nothing for tourists,' he says with a modesty that surprises me. 'No, no. Just a local beauty salon.' Thanks to his work at the hotel, he now speaks English. He sits down on my bed and we reminisce about the islands, about old Abdul Jemal, about the policeman's daughter on Sapuka Island. He also remembers the mosque on a little island, Kubang Lemari, where we bathed in the fountain to wash off salt that had accumulated during two weeks at sea, astonishing the local population with the soapy foam we created. He brings me up to date on Pa-Suni, the captain, who now lives on the tiny island of Sakenan, which can be reached on foot at low tide. We reminisce, but our hearts aren't in it; the future is limited for both of us. And the girl of Lombok, who died of love as the wind carried to her ears the sound of flutes played by her betrothed, who had been killed in Java. 'He is playing for me,' she said. That was seven years ago, that was in another life.

In those days, I continually travelled through the mirror, living first on one side and then on the other. That resulted in a certain schizophrenia. One day, Idanna disappeared, I don't know from which side of the mirror.

'We must go to see Pa-Suni right away.'

We hoist the sail of a *jukung*, and a gust of wind carries us to Sakenan Island. Pa-Suni has not yet returned from his night of fishing, and we wait for him on a bamboo platform, drinking black coffee with lots of sugar.

Pa-Suni is a true captain: he shows no surprise whatsoever at seeing me, and a good hour goes by before he asks me any questions about my eyes. In the meantime, I ask him:

'What about your ship, the *Labuan Sinar*?'

'Suda rusak – shot to hell already.'

'And your father-in-law, old Abdul Jemal?'

'Suda mati – dead already.'

'Ah, and your wife?'

'Suda mati. Sekarang saja orang meskin – I am now a poor man. Do you remember that you promised me an underwater floodlight for fishing at night? Sekarang hidup sukar – life is hard these days. To find fish, you have to go far out, and my boat is too small.'

At three o'clock in the morning, in the bay of Alas, it is dark and the ship's deck resounds with the sailors' hurried footsteps. Pa-Suni gives brief orders. The wind has come up; we must take advantage of it and set out. It's a good wind. Soon a faint shudder comes from behind the volcano. It is dawn breaking, and the *Labuan Sinar*, her sails in full bloom, leans at just the right angle as she elegantly speeds to its encounter. Watching the world come to life, the sailors are silent. Only the orders of Pa-Suni, the best captain in the Celebes Sea, can be heard.

That was seven years ago.

'Buy a boat, and I will get together the best crew. I know all the islands, the whole sea; we can do some trading that will

bring in money. Ado! Banyak wang. I want to get married again.'
He laughs, cynically. He doubts that with my dead eyes I'll really
want to go back to sea. I think things over, I think that, in any
case, the past cannot be recaptured, and that it's better to turn
your back on it, brutally.

TWENTY-EIGHT

I must get away from this deserted hotel and beach where there is still a chance of my meeting Valushka. I am too aware of the sadness in her voice when she cried, 'Go away from me. Please!' I am going to hide among the rice paddies, in the village of Sidakaria, at my friend Putu Swarsa's, and I'll stay there until her presence no longer haunts the Island. Ida Bagus, the one-eyed Brahmin's son who works in the little hotel where she is staying, will be my eyes.

Already Putu Swarsa is waiting for me on his motorbike. I throw my things together and leave my mouldy room as I would a nightmare. The motor starts up with a crash, and before I can even think about what I am doing, I find myself clinging with one hand to Putu's belt and to my luggage with the other. We race down a winding road through the rice paddies to the village. The wind cleanses me of my sweat.

Tomorrow will be Kuningan, the harvest festival. The houses resonate with the sounds of turtles being hacked to pieces in preparation for the sacred feast. I listen to the people in this little village of Sidakaria; they were born there, they will die there. They will be burned there by their children, for whom destiny promises the same. I listen to Putu laughing with his three-year-old son, who will be responsible for his cremation. Certainly, evenings are a little monotonous in the village, and everyone dreams of faraway cities. Here the houses are built upon ancestors' ashes, and beyond them, beyond the luxurious gardens, lie the rice paddies, which, no matter what, will protect them, and their children, and their children's children, as it did their fathers' fathers.

Gradually a long-forgotten calm returns to the village, all is silent for a time, and then music begins to fill the air. Bamboo music, gamelan music, flute music, and the birds.

Why have I stayed? I suspect that, subconsciously, I believe that it is here that I will see again. On this island, the colours and images are more vivid than anywhere else and the horizon has a gentler curve. I want to believe that those images, being stronger here, will pierce my blindness; and in fact, as the days go by, they do begin to emerge. I allow my mind to be invaded by thousands of bits of information. Sounds, smells, the feel of things, the voices of the Island people, and my memory of the past do not fail to move me in the end. I see the rice paddies, I see the hills, I see the sea. The tombs have sunk into the past to which they belong. Gradually confidence returns and life flows gently.

And, as always, when life resumes, what one encounters is death. One night, the howling of dogs envelops the village. They are howling at death, at the imminent death of the sea, down by Kampung Bugis, where the river, sickened by the mud of the rice paddies, vomits into a salt-whitened lagoon. A night stabbed by stars besieges the rooftops. We huddle up around a wood fire, which incenses the air in silence. At this meeting place of two worlds, I am filled alternately with anguish and hope, emptiness and mystery. A tree trembles although there is not a breath of wind, as if shrugging its shoulders at astonishing thoughts. Suddenly, from the dirt road that goes through the village comes the trampling of bare feet. People are walking in silence. Putu Swarsa is softly playing his guitar and his cousin Madé is singing. At the other end of the village, the howling of the dogs becomes distressingly high-pitched. Putu stops playing.

'Someone has died. They have just brought him to the cemetery to wait for his cremation. He was young; that's why the dogs are howling so loudly.'

The air is so thick that it's hard to swallow. The wind seems to carry the cackling of Rangda the witch as she tears the great blue lotus to pieces with her teeth.

'Let's go to a *warong* and have a glass of arak,' says Cousin

Madé, whose nickname is 'Sticky' because girls stick to him like doves to birdlime.

Putu, who stays behind, gives him some advice which I cannot hear. The motorbike starts up, and the cool air immediately relaxes me. All of a sudden, the motor coughs three times and stalls. Madé jumps off and starts pushing the bike as fast as he can, making loud but unintelligible noises. I have just enough time to grab onto the back seat and follow, running after him. At last, several hundred feet farther on, he stops, out of breath, starts the motor up again, and takes off without answering my question. The answer doesn't come until he has a glass of arak before him.

'Putu told me, "Don't pass by the cemetery. The death is too recent; the spirit is still restless." But I am lazy, and to by-pass the cemetery I would have had to go out of my way. Sure enough, right there in front of the cemetery, the dead man stopped my motorbike.'

He is laughing now, because on the Island spirits are just as playful as the living, and he turns his attention towards the girl who has brought us the arak. I can tell from the sound of his voice, like a timid tiger's, that the *jegeg* is beautiful.

From time to time, we go swimming near the temple of Merta Sari, where the beach curves gently and where the calm sea, lazily heated by the sun, allows long, immersed conversations. One day, an Australian voice tells me:

'My name is Bret. What's it like making love when you're blind? Excuse me. May I introduce myself?'

He takes my hand and runs it through his hair, which is curly and thick.

'There are all kinds of stories about you here on the Island.'

'I'm not interested.'

'Some say they cut off your cock. Others say you're part of the Mafia and they were taking revenge. Now that I see you, I don't believe any of it. Too bad!'

He laughs. And then, for an hour, he describes everything that's going on: the children I hear laughing, how the light plays on the water that they splash at each other, a mauve sail gliding along, linking the cobalt blue of the sea to the azure sky, and the vanishing of the little island of Sakenan into the mist as the sun climbs higher and higher. I listen to his description. He organises space, distributes colours, attributes values. Bret is a painter, and Whitley is a prestigious signature in New York, London, and Sydney. He has the kind of painter's eye that moves first from the inside towards the outside, then beyond. Anyone who looks at a painting moves from the outside to the inside; in both cases, it is essential to be able to see beyond objects, faces, landscapes. With Bret, the inner image imposes itself. He not only sees the outside world, he creates it.

Most people don't go beyond the obvious and have no inner image. For instance, if I ask:

'What's that?'

'A palace.'

'What do I hear?'

'Musicians.'

'Are there many of them?'

'Quite a few.'

That can be called looking at the world without expecting anything from it. Actually, we were in front of the palace of Gianyar, which is bustling with activity because Raka's brother, whom I haven't seen for seven years, is getting married. I would only find out about it the following day from local gossip.

When Bret describes life to me, he paints, first with large brush strokes and then, for details he considers more significant, with a fine sable brush. Sometimes he takes hold of my finger and makes it trace in space the composition of the landscape before us. In his hand my finger becomes a paintbrush. And still, as intensely alive as Bret is, he also makes me face death. On the beach he tells me:

'Jo is going to die. That's why we all came here. My wife, my daughter, Jo's wife, his daughter, and two other friends as well. Jo is a sculptor, thirty-one years old, and the doctors say there's no hope. He is completely ravaged by cancer. They have given him one or two months to live. We have been here for four weeks. Jo is my only friend; he is more to me than a brother. Come see him.'

I go two days later to a little hotel that was built during the period of Dutch colonisation. Jo slipped into a coma the previous evening. His wife ran to the big tourist hotel, where two hundred Australian doctors were holding a convention. She went up to the speakers' platform and said, 'Please help me. My husband is dying of terminal cancer. I don't want him to suffer. Help me.' There was an embarrassed silence. Not one of them got up. Finally they realised that it was the famous sculptor Jo G. and that at his bedside was the notorious artist Bret Whitley. Whereupon they eagerly rushed forward to offer their services. Too late. One of their company, a perfectly modest little doctor who had only a vague sense of the art world, had already gone to see the patient. He did not even leave his name.

I stay in this little colonial hotel for two weeks, somehow unable to leave. Perhaps I am held here by this continuing drama, this approaching death. Every day Jo is less and less aware of what is going on. The pain is sometimes unbearable. Fortunately, heroin has been brought in from Sydney by doctor's prescription. It is added to his intravenous solution. He has lost his hair, his eyelashes, his eyebrows. Everything has been burned away by the cobalt. That's as it was when he came to the Island, but then he was still on his feet. Now he is bedridden. A week ago, he ordered a suit, had chisels and some stone brought in. 'When I'm better, I'll do something with them.' And yet the doctors have told him, 'There is no hope.'

I hear Zahava, his eight-year-old daughter, playing under the shower with some little girls who peddle sea shells on the beach. 'My daddy is very sick, but he's going to get well.' His body slowly becomes an empty shell. The women spend their days and nights washing him, changing the sheets, keeping him cool, trying to make his death more gentle. It's hard to say if he is even conscious of all this. As though hypnotised, paralysed with pain, Bret cannot stop sketching his friend's face. His drawings vibrate with so much love that even those foolish enough to find his work inappropriate say nothing.

Finally, one night, at three o'clock, what little is left of Jo's body stops breathing. 'Jo is dead.' We hear the words and feel nothing but a strange void. Bret says to me:

'The terrifying thing is that all of a sudden, there was nothing in the room anymore. He was dead, completely dead. Nothing went anywhere. The room suddenly was empty.'

At dawn, under a pavilion near the shore, Anna tells Zahava about her father's death. The child is sitting in her mother's lap, arms and legs wrapped around her.

'No, Zahava, he won't get well. He is dead. He can't get better anymore.'

And the child does not cry, refusing to understand.

'But what if we have very good medicine brought from Australia?'

'He is dead, Zahava.'

She doesn't completely understand the meaning of this word until later in the afternoon. In the morgue, her father's body has been placed in a coffin filled with ice cubes, which Zahava helps Anna to replace as they melt. In this country of cremations, no one has thought to equip the morgue with refrigeration.

And, as always happens on this island when such forces are unleashed, their spiralling motion cannot be checked. At seven o'clock on the same morning, Putu Swarsa arrives on his motorbike and hands me a telegram. I ask him to read it: 'Odile is dead. Stop. Car accident.' My sister-in-law, whom I loved dearly, is dead, leaving three little boys. It's a terrible blow, and I feel my heart tightening, tightening. The tears streaming from beneath the steel are wiped away by a hotel employee with a roll of toilet paper. He does this gravely and methodically. I am not aware of any of this; Bret tells me about it later.

'I must go throw myself into the sea.'

I must go and wash in the sea, wash away all the sorrow that is suffocating me. Wash away death, all these deaths. I feel that life is at low tide. I must do something to destroy death, to annihilate it; I must do something to prove that I am alive.

A hand, 'the Hand', takes mine and leads me to the beach. In the water our arms meet, as do our legs, our bodies. I am warmed by her blood, by her life. She calms my panic. Intertwined with her, I cry and plunge my head into the sea. I do not want to hear of death any longer. I would like to kill Death.

TWENTY-NINE

Every morning 'the Hand' leads me to the same marble table under the pavilion by the Java Sea. On this particular morning, someone is strolling along the beach, drawing plaintive music from a makeshift violin. The repetitive melody passes and fades away, sadly, so sadly, until it is engulfed by the sound of the waves and children's laughter.

I will go back to Honfleur in September and look at the sea in the golden sunlight, sitting beneath an old-fashioned pavilion. I will never see Honfleur again, or the face of the woman I love, or the expressions of my mother as she grows older. I will never see anything again. How can one survive this? How can anyone get used to this obscurity, this monotonous darkness? This shore, black with boredom. They ask me whether I'm getting used to it, or assure me that I will, little by little. Deep within me, I cry out, 'Never!' I must never get used to it and forget what I was, for that is surely more authentically myself than what they have made of me. This is irrevocable, but it is not me.

I am writing these lines under this pavilion on a beach. I hear the sea and the children. It makes no difference that this is the Java Sea, not the English Channel, that the pavilion is made of bamboo rather than of elaborate pine. I am writing these lines, as I did at the hospital, using a piece of cardboard that I position on the paper so that I can follow the edge with my pen. The only problem with this system is that the tails of letters like *p*, *q*, *g*, and *j* bump up against the cardboard and don't end up on the page. The work is slow and at times fills me with despair, but I need to tell what has happened to me, what is happening to me now, because it concerns all of us. The violence of which

I was a victim is repeated in the same way every night in New York and, for the most part, everywhere around the world. It is a violence fueled by personal or governmental whim; it is meant to satisfy men's appetites or their ideologies. Hate has always intrigued me, particularly the hate men have for one another.

At about the age of fourteen, I read the first eyewitness accounts of the death camps in Nazi Germany. It was both horrifying and fascinating to discover as a child that the adult world was not a rational one. What particularly interested me were prisoners' accounts. I could feel within myself the courage of one as well as the abjectness of another. I was both of those prisoners. I tried to imagine how I would react. I pictured myself betraying my comrades for a morsel of bread or resisting and being tortured to death without speaking. I don't mean that my situation attains the same degree of horror as a death-camp prisoner's. I am not in danger of dying. I simply want to testify.

No, I don't want to get used to this, and I struggle so that I will not be overwhelmed by the invisible. Every day, I force my brain to perceive visually. Since I can't constantly ask questions, I arbitrarily assign colors to flowers, to taxis, to women's hair, to sarongs, to dogs. When I think back over a certain event, a certain day in the hills, I have to make an effort to remember that I didn't actually see it, that it was only imagined. Sometimes the memory of an event is so visual that I place it in the past, before the attack. How can I believe that I have never seen Valushka? I know every square inch of her body, the exact sheen of her hair, the texture of her skin, the beauty spot in the hollow of her spine, the perfection of her sex. But above all, I know exactly the expression in her eyes, a vivacity veiled with sadness. In her Russian soul I see, although it is invisible to others, from what they say, the negative poetry of everyday life. It is impossible for me to trust anyone else. She is brunette, red-headed, blond, beautiful, ordinary, cute, slender, heavy. Someone said to me, 'One wonders why such a beautiful girl should get involved with someone who can't see her.' But others have said, 'At least now he doesn't have to worry about women's beauty.' Wrong! Now I am more concerned with beauty than ever before, it would annoy me to have people think, 'Fortunately, he can't see her.' I do perceive beauty.

I know that a certain sort of magic would emanate from Valushka when she came near me or when we walked down the streets of New York together, so sure of ourselves. Her beauty bathed us in a magnetic halo. There was no danger of bumping against a curb or of falling into the gutter; it was a perfect dance. Passers-by would turn around, without understanding. There was something strange about us, but they didn't know what. People who saw us then described it to me later, after getting to know me.

And how can I get used to anything when there is this beast lurking deep within me? This beast which is blindness itself. Not physical blindness, which is a mere mechanical accident that prevents images from reaching the brain, but the psychic blindness brought about by that privation. This beast which must be tamed every morning, pitilessly, as soon as I wake up, so that it won't invade my day.

The Island is buffeted by trade winds and storms. At night, short-lived but violent rains batter the ylang-ylang roof and wake me up. Here, people shut themselves in at night. They barricade themselves in for protection from evil spirits as much as from prowlers. Two weeks ago, a man was murdered, stabbed to death. I wouldn't like to become obsessed with the idea of being attacked, but I am aware of a certain fear, which I can no longer ignore. In New York, when I went home alone at night, the slightest sound behind me would tie my stomach in knots, humiliate me. That pernicious acid continues to eat its way into my heart. In the darkness of this room at the other end of the world, I live through the attack again, listening to the sounds distorted by the wind.

This morning, the Island is calm. The wind has died down and Ramadan came to an end yesterday. Even though Islam is not the religion of the Island, everything comes to a halt during these three days of celebration ending the fasting, for it is the religion of the civil servants. Even the waves, in spite of the rising tide, mix their silver and gold with a new laziness. I have abandoned my pavilion to plunge deeper into the forgotten regions of the Island, where there is probably nothing to be seen except the monotonous repetition of palm trees, there where the wind blows straight in from the open sea. Birds sing, crickets chirp, the air is filled with the scents of flowers, grass, and seaweed. There is no means of public transportation here. To leave my new house I must hitch a ride on the back of a motorbike or rent one of the mini-trucks that take the place of public transport. This part of the Island is such a dead end, culminating in the stagnant water of a lagoon, that seven years ago I hadn't bothered to explore it.

The fact is that, as I write these lines, only a three-day sail separates me from Makassar. In the evening, a wind blows from over there and enters my house. It whips the darkness across my face, forcing itself into my lungs. Laden with everything it has picked up over there, it is a dangerous, violent, immense force, and it paralyses me. Temptation and terror. Will I ever go to Java again? The wind answers me: Never again.

Along the beach the butterflies are in mourning. Love has vanished. This evening the night is so black that I could gather it up and give it to you; the wind blows music over the hills of the Island. I search in the sand for your footprint, but the wind, the waves, have wiped everything away. In my heart there is neither wind nor wave. I love you and yet the sand has become black. A volcano has erupted and poured out its lava. My love is like the sea, limitless. But this evening it is like a grain of sand, lost on the beach. There is a bird singing in the very heart of the night, making me think of you. There is this bird that refuses to believe in the night. Its song is like a flower, mauve and red and pink, opening up in the darkness. It is the heart of the night. It is your heart. The imminence of the monsoon casts a spell of melancholy. Already the wind is heavy with chagrin and my thoughts grow mouldy. The sea is losing patience; it begins to roar threateningly. I must exorcise the chagrin, the melancholy, the rain. In the middle of the night, a man shouted out there in the direction of the sea, but the wind swept everything away. I don't know whether his shout was love or death. My heart is like a cat; it can see at night. And this evening it sees only you. In this house at the tip of the Island, amid the sea, the wind, and the volcanoes, your spirit echoes as if it were in a sea conch. Boats have come to the shore by my house and have gone off again without me. You loved me, and you have gone off without me. From these stagnant waters, the wind carries the scent of dead loves from the silt of forgotten lagoons.

The Island has fallen prey to mosquitoes and an intense humidity. In the evening, the wind from the open sea no longer wafts through my house; it has turned towards the northeast and three volcanoes stand in its path. My solitude, coupled with my work in digging up and writing down recollections I have worked so hard to bury, creates a tension that is difficult to relieve. I listen to cassette tapes I recorded in my hospital bed and at the rehabilitation centre. The recent past, this part of me that is already dead, resurfaces. On the tape my voice sounds different as I grew more hopeful or more desperate. I listen uneasily to that exhibition of self; it's like having your handwriting analysed. How I would like to pick up a book tonight and lose myself in something else. The air is absolutely motionless and the sea silent. The nights are moonless; no bird sings. At infrequent intervals, pale light flashes through my eyelids and muffled rumblings roll in from the direction of the volcanoes. But the rain refuses to fall. I am suffocating under the mosquito netting. The sound of a motor approaches slowly on the uneven dirt road. A door slams. I hear voices. Ketut Ketchil, who takes the place of Désirée in this house, comes into my room.

'Some friends have arrived. Orang besar. Munkin, orang australia. There is a tall man, perhaps an Australian.'

He sounds suspicious, since he knows that I don't care very much for unexpected visitors. But this evening I am glad to escape the silence, this confrontation with myself. I hardly know the people who are inviting me to dinner. We drive inland, leaving dirt roads for asphalt. Dogs bark as our car passes.

On a veranda overlooking a garden, people are talking slowly, in tired voices. The smell of ganja cigarettes floats in the air with the scent of burned grass; a German, some Italians, an Algerian, a Frenchwoman – migratory birds. Goa, Kuta, Nepal . . . their lives move to the rhythm of the monsoons. I am served a plate of spaghetti and a mushroom omelet. A man sits down next to me and asks me questions, but I don't understand everything he says. He has a strange accent. I am quickly growing bored. I'd like to go home. Suddenly my head begins to throb. My thoughts start racing and, within a few minutes, they are flying at a thousand miles an hour. My veins boil with energy. The mushrooms in the omelet were hallucinogenic. The man goes on talking about creativity, about how impossible it is to choose. 'If I choose, I cut myself off from everything else.' These hallucinogens invade every part of my head, leaving no room for patience and tolerance. He keeps on talking without realising that danger.

'You understand, with women it's the same thing; choosing one means cutting yourself off from the others. I came here to run away from twelve women, ha, ha, ha! What do you think of that?'

The mushrooms prompt me to say:

'I think that's bullshit! But that doesn't make any difference. We all talk nonsense now and then. What matters is knowing that you're doing it.'

But he doesn't agree with me at all.

'You don't understand. The point is to keep creativity alive.'

'No, no. The point is lying to yourself more or less success-fully.'

Those damn mushrooms won't let go of me. Everyone joins in. High-flown ideas chewed over by mediocre minds. They would all like to be reassured, but a demon drives me to destroy their self-satisfaction. They lose patience with me. Enraged, the German tells me:

'Go get rid of your blind man's frustrations somewhere else. Take him out on the road, maybe a truck will run him over.'

I jump up. 'The Hand' gives me my cane and her hand. And that is the end of my brief acquaintance with this band of gnomes.

The motorbike races towards the hills where the air is cooler.

I ride upon the sound of flutes which propel me, dispersing me among the leaves of the huge trees above us. And you, girl of the hills, I straddle your motorbike, which explodes like a gamelan to the rhythm of your laughter. We plunge into the heat of the night; the chirping of crickets blends in with the croaking of frogs and toads, pretending it is broad daylight in the dark rice paddies. And my roaring heart races. The flute pierces the moon. My roots strangle my soul, for man's feet are made for running, not for being planted in the earth. True, this flute in the hills may not be sufficient, but it is honest, certainly as good as words. It takes me above myself. Without it, one forgets that the night can be so deep, that the sky can be so boundlessly resonant, and that a gaze can stretch towards the ends of the earth. What celestial vault shelters this island where the flutes dare bring love and death together?

THIRTY

On this island where the air is limp with humidity, I am sometimes afraid that my heart is growing mouldy, but in fact the struggle against decay is won every day. Like a fish stranded on the shore, I plunge back into the sea, which the full moon brings surging up almost beneath my bed. My knees and spine have been loosened up by daily swimming in the reef-protected sea. My limbs have been stretched out. The sea is the only element in which I feel free – no walls, no trees, no holes. Nothing to collide with or fall over. I swim with my head under water, having nothing to look at. I feel the strength of currents, the difference in temperatures. The water gets warmer as I approach the beach. As I move towards the open sea, the coral reef rumbles. Near the shore, there is the perpetual breaking of the waves. Between these two sounds, I move along either perpendicular or parallel lines. And then there is the position of the sun, which I note very carefully through my joined eyelids before diving into the water. Drifting along on my back, I relax completely as the sun pours down on my face.

Kayan, the fisherman who takes me along on his *jukung* to catch fish out beyond the reef, comes one morning with a wind surfer. He shows me how to keep my balance, then how to lean into the wind. He is very patient and I am persistent; being swept along by the wind fills me with a heady feeling of freedom. After three days, I manage a few hundred yards without falling head first into the sail or flat on my back into the water. The wind blows steadily from Sakenan Island. I grasp the sail firmly and laugh when I hear Kayan shout:

'Watch where you're going!'

This is precisely the problem. How can I stay on course?

Naturally, there is the direction of the wind and the angle of the sail, but at such a speed and with a changing wind, those indications are not reliable. What I need is a speaking compass that I could wear strapped around my head. An audible signal on my forehead would alert me to whether I was veering to the left or to the right; by keeping this sound constant, I would be able to stay on course. Such a compass would also make it possible for me to steer the *jukung* without too much trouble. I will have to find an electrician who can make one for me. I am sure it can be done.

The rainy season has arrived, with all its humidity and heat. The mattress is damp; the sheets smell of mildew. A veil of sweat covers my skin, the sweat of a full moon. Here, it doesn't smell sour; it tastes rather sweet as it forms beads on my upper lip and trickles into my mouth. Like a fragrant balm, it saturates my skin. True, I can no longer fall asleep between Valushka's ballerina's thighs; this flesh has left me a widower; she no longer teases me with remarks like 'Close your eyes and go to sleep.' But however tumultuous the nights may be, the flame she has lighted in me has never completely gone out, and I am no longer the prey of darkness. This love is intact at the core of my being, ready to warm me. I am no longer the same. My inner life is serene; the panic has faded and I can reflect calmly, with greater concentration.

During the night, after the rain, giant frogs have added their oboes to the flute of an unknown bird. Through my eyelids, my mind is illuminated by flashes of lightning. Little by little, evenings have become different, and failure, though always present to some extent, is retreating.

The rumbling of the reef has ceased; the sea is at high tide. It must be about midnight. Something drives me outdoors. The sea breeze refreshes me. The path alongside the house draws me towards the beach. I splash through big puddles still warm from a full day of sun. The sea, smooth as a mirror, gently laps the shore. I imagine the phosphorescent strip of plankton and, beyond the reef, out on the open sea, Pa-Suni fishing in his miserable little boat. After two or three visits, he has never come back to see me. He, too, does not believe in the past. Sitting on the sand, I listen to the music of the gamelan in the hills, the honking of horns, roosters crowing from kampong to kampong, the roaring of motorbikes as they race towards temples quaking with the ringing of gongs, and the pervasive, solitary trills of the birds. All this hubbub of full moon. Today is *bulan purnama*.

Time has passed, imperceptibly. To return home, I take a shortcut through a palm grove towards a footpath that I am familiar with, leading up to the temple of Merta Sari. The silence is complete. The moon must have set. The only sound is my cane slashing through the tall grass. I advance, and suddenly I have the feeling I am deep in unknown territory. But what can I do except continue along until I run across another path? At my side, the brutal howling of a dog sends my heart into my throat. A second later, I hear the whole yapping pack. I must be near some houses. The dogs are all around me, silent. As soon as I make a move, the howling begins again. Shivers run up and down my spine. Fear, animal fear and the humiliation of not being able to control it. The pack barks; their prey is in sight. The stag tires, panics. I start walking straight ahead, swinging my cane about wildly, too quickly. The pack follows. I run into a thick hedge, change direction, run into another hedge a hundred feet farther on. I realise that I am caught in an enclosed field. Without knowing it, I must have wandered behind the lagoon, where there is a very poor community which lives off the sea and whatever washes up on the shore, as well as a few basic crops. The rest of the Island considers these people to be primitive, crude, superstitious. Is some frightened peasant going to beat me to death with his nail-studded club? I drive my way through the hedge and fall into a ditch, climb back up, and find myself on another path. The dogs are still barking but are no longer following me. I keep moving forward, quickly, on the level ground. I wander about for three hours like this, stumbling through villages, rousing hordes of dogs, which I keep at a distance by flicking my cigarette lighter. Gradually my fear disappears. Near a house, I call out, 'Hello! Ada orang disini? Hello, please!' It has become clear that their superstitions will protect me. I will not be attacked, but I won't be helped, either. I am the king of the night, the strange creature Rangda or the Barong. People are bolting their doors. Terrified, they remain transfixed on their bamboo beds, listening. Only a bird goes on singing its solitary song, undisturbed by me. I walk through the hamlets without slowing down. I sense their nearness even before the sleeping dogs wake and confirm the existence of human dwellings. They are like a dense presence beneath the palm trees, announced sometimes by the smell of cold smoke or the sound of cows brought in for the night. I advance rapidly, feeling a real sense of pleasure now. My cane strikes the ground with a steady rhythm. I am not heading anywhere. I don't know how many times I have taken a different path, changed my direction. Far off, sometimes on my right, sometimes on my left, the sea roars. I try to keep it behind me so that I can find the asphalt road to Kuta. All of a sudden, the path is interrupted by a heap of pebbles. I don't understand. Should I turn back? I am tired, exhausted. I am getting blisters from clutching my cane. I climb up on a heap of coral, explore the other side with my cane. It gives off a hard sound. A kind of platform. A lime kiln? A construction site? I step forward with a bare foot. It is hot, it is hard, it is familiar. It's the asphalt of the road to Kuta.

Feeling proud, joyful, relieved, I now stride briskly ahead. Surely the big tourist hotel can't be far off. I'll soon hear it's generator. A motorbike comes towards me and stops.

'I know you. Climb on. I'm going fishing right in front of your house.'

'But this isn't the right direction . . . Or is it? Where am I?'

'Jallan Baru Nusa Dua.'

I am three or four miles from my house. All I had wanted to do was go home, twenty-five yards from where I was sitting on the beach.

Its remote location and the absence of any direct route to it mean that few people manage to come as far as the house. Practically the only ones who do are women from Sakenan Island who disembark on the beach in the morning and, chattering all the while, disappear into the palm grove, balancing huge enamel bowls filled with fish on their heads. They're on their way to sell the night's catch in the Denpasar market.

However, one day I hear footsteps on the veranda in front of my room. I go out and ask:

'Who's there?' No answer. 'Siapa?' Still nothing, except for the sound of breathing on my left. I am getting angry. 'When you go into somebody's house, you at least say hello!'

In the garden I hear Ketut Ketchil's racing steps.

'Tuan! Tuan! It's my sister. She can't answer you, she's mute.'

And then there's an Italian writer who comes by, a friend of Albert Camus.

'I'm tired now. No, I don't mean tired of life, but of writing. It's just too tiring.'

I listen to the weary voice of this solitary man, who is well into his fifties. I sense that he looks at the world, and at me, with great intensity but with little tenderness.

'I'll be frank with you. I'm a racist. It's hell here, a joke. They're monkeys; even sexually, they don't interest me.'

As I listen, I hear the voice of a man alone with his intelligence and his culture. He was in Vietnam during the war with American soldiers 'who would go off and fight eight hours a day, just like going to the office.' And then he was with the Vietcong. He covered most of the Ho Chi Minh trail on foot, escorted by a hundred Vietcong. 'I got fucking bored.' His articles were published in Hanoi and Moscow. That was ten years ago, seven years ago. During the same period, I also witnessed the war. I was in Saigon a few weeks before the final collapse. He, too, saw all the oil reserves of South Vietnam and Cambodia go up in flames, covering Saigon with such a black cloud that everyone who had one took his umbrella along.

'It's a real joke here, and besides, I don't like religious states. Things always go better in secular states. After D'Annunzio was blinded in an airplane accident, he used two wooden rulers to guide his writing. What do you do?'

'I use the edge of a thick piece of cardboard. I've tried the rulers, but I feel uncomfortable writing between two sticks of wood.'

'What about books?'

'For the time being, I'm not reading at all. Perhaps it's not such a bad thing. I used to read too much.'

'So I suppose talking has become essential?'

'And listening.'

'Ah, yes. Other people's words are often more important than books.'

'So what do you think the solution is for Southeast Asia?'

'Colonialism. But a much more drastic colonialism than the kind we have seen so far – a Japanese colonialism. I have just come from Japan, and it has deeply affected me. A real culture, and this obsession with harmony and efficiency!'

I feel the sadness in his humour. It is difficult for me to find any sincerity in the soulful outpourings of this disillusioned, old-school European. But this man does more than see; he looks.

'I am condemned to look,' he complains.

'In his play *No Exit*, Sartre specified in the stage directions that the actors have no eyelids. In this hell they are condemned to look – to look at others watching them.'

'That's right – that's the way it is.'

'With me, it's just the opposite. My eyelids have been sewn shut.'

'Is that a relief?'

'In some ways, yes, but above all I feel how relieved others are not to be observed, or seen at all.'

And with one last tragicomical paradox, he went on his way, like some character out of the commedia dell'arte.

This morning there's a good wind for trolling. With Kayan the fisherman, I slide the *jukung* to the water's edge. The *jukung* is a small dugout canoe with two lateral outriggers and a short Arabian sail. As soon as we leave the protection of the coast, we are assailed by violent gusts of wind. Before long, I feel the boat rising and falling inside great hollow pockets formed by waves 'as big as a house,' as Kayan describes them. The wind is howling in my ears, changing its pitch every time I turn my head. I hear the bamboo outriggers and the mast cracking.

Terror fills me. It seems that, at any moment, the entire rig is
going to collapse, to break into pieces, and go shooting off into
the wind. The waves slap my face and engulf the dugout. I bail
at full speed. Although the sea fills the tree trunk as fast as I
can empty it, I bail and bail, glad to have something to do. Kayan
cries out. Just as the boat begins to plunge from the crest of
another wave, a blast of wind rips the mast out of its socket.
Kayan steps over me. I hold onto the tiller. The waves get
stronger and stronger, and I hear the groaning of the reef getting
dangerously close. Kayan takes over the tiller, saying, 'It's too
late to change tack; we'd capsize. We have got to cross the
reef.' I latch onto every sound. I'm petrified, I've got to admit,
and it annoys me. Seven years ago, on this same sea, a whirlwind
tore out our mast, and we were finally washed up on an island
of lepers. Neither the tornado nor the lepers frightened me
then, but now a simple squall is enough to tie my stomach in
knots. The difference isn't so much that I'm blind now, but that,
seven years ago, I felt invulnerable. Yes, invulnerable, as old
Abdul Jemal had said I was when I met him on that little island
of Pulau Kahung, to which he had come sixty-five years earlier
from far-off Egypt. He had become blind as a result of a spell
cast on him by one of his enemies. 'I have populated this island
myself!' he would say, striking his balls with his fist. 'Take him
with you on your boat,' he had told his son-in-law, pointing to
me. 'Nothing can happen to him.' And when I went off that night
to be alone and unwittingly ended up falling asleep in a place
where they buried the dead, the old soothsayer repeated to
Pa-Suni:

'Leave me alone; I told you nothing can happen to him.'

Those words, which a little boy reported to me, stayed with
me throughout the whole voyage.

But now I know that I am vulnerable. I feel it just as acutely
as I did when I visited the Jesuits on Park Avenue. I feel like an
Achilles who doesn't know where his heel is. As I continue to
bail, I begin to wonder whether this condition isn't in fact
preferable. Kayan told me later, 'If you could have seen how
high the waves were, you wouldn't have been so calm.'

Three successive breakers flood the boat as the rudder

struggles against the wind. The water and the air are pushing in opposite directions, one against the hull and the other against the sail. Everything is cracking, and I can feel the bench I am sitting on being wrenched into a diagonal position. Will the outriggers hold up? I anchor the bailing scoop with my foot and cling to the side of the boat.

We have crossed over. Only the boom has been torn out of its socket and one of the sail pins has come loose. Under the direction of Kayan, who is himself busy with the tiller, I repair the sail. On this side of the coral reef the hollows formed by the waves are deeper, but since they are wider the boat is not tossed about so violently. We change tack. While Kayan struggles against the wind to position the Arabian sail, the boat fills with water. If it were to fill up, it would be so heavy that the mast would break and the outriggers come apart. I push the tiller completely off to one side and let the sail unfurl. I must act quickly so that I can get back to bailing.

'Grab the sheet!' shouts Kayan, his voice rising and falling somewhere above my head.

By all means, but he's completely forgetting that I can't see anything at all, and it's not really an appropriate time to point this out to him.

'The sheet, where is it?'

'There, there!'

He must be pointing to it. Let's keep calm.

'To the left or to the right?'

But the wind, the waves, the flapping sail, and more than anything else the thundering reef are so deafening that I can't make out what Kayan is shouting. Finally, starting from the mast and feeling my way along the boom, I locate the sheet. I do it very quickly so that I won't have to leave the tiller unattended very long. I can tell from the fisherman's voice that this is no joke, and I begin to long to return home.

Now we are heading back. Kayan has taken the tiller and is trying to cross back over the reef at a familiar point, but the wind is so strong that our keelless boat, made only for coastal fishing, is forced off course. I start rowing in an attempt to keep the boat from drifting; at the same time I try to move with the wave that is carrying us along. The boat is suddenly lifted up, and its bow takes an almost vertical plunge. If the outriggers, which are longer than the dugout, are driven into the coral, we've had it. In three seconds, the boat is lifted up vertically and carried to the other side of the reef. The waves, which are smaller but choppier now, assail us mercilessly and I go on bailing relentlessly. At last we reach the beach, where other fishermen surround us, shouting:

'Bodoh! Bodoh! Idiots . . .'

Then, noticing that Kayan's mate can't see anything, they burst out laughing.

Alone in my room, I listen to the blood coursing through my veins and, rising from the depth of my stomach, laughter takes the place of fear. I hear Aho mutter:

'What nonsense! What a silly thing to do! So you have to go and risk breaking your neck just to feel better! How childish.'

But I can tell from his voice that he isn't angry. And because I have been afraid of drowning, afraid of not staying alive, I am now less afraid of rotting away.

THIRTY-ONE

Six months have passed already since I arrived on the Island. Immigration points this out to me; I had not really been keeping track. In their precise, punctilious way, the Moslem civil servants have notified me that I can't stay here any longer without getting my visa renewed abroad. The nearest place is Singapore.

So here I am sitting in the little airport with a certain uneasiness and a ticket for Singapore. A certain uneasiness because no one will be waiting for me when I arrive. The plane is late and the waiting room is buzzing with foreign languages: Italians, Australians, Germans, Frenchmen – all kinds of noisy, excited, sunburned, confused tourists. The women's voices are shriller than usual, as if they were addressing the whole crowd. Liberated from the confinement of their everyday life, they are possessed by an exhibitionistic frenzy. The men, on the contrary, speak with deeper voices and behave like male archetypes, the masters of adventure. A man sits down beside me, asks for a light, and immediately launches into the story of his life. I listen, intrigued, to this living book being opened before me. He is an Australian travelling with his wife. His profession: fashion designer, with several stores in Melbourne. From his voice I can tell he's not involved in trends; he simply dresses people, and business is obviously good. But the accent? 'I was born in Poland,' meaning that he is a Jew. And the heart of the book appears. My only interruptions are to ask about specific dates and places: at thirteen the ghetto, at fourteen the work camp, at fifteen the concentration camp, Treblinka, hunger. His job: holding an SS officer's mirror every morning while he shaved. All he had to his name was a little war treasure, if one can call it that: ten cigarettes. One morning he offered two to the officer without asking for anything in return. The officer had a sandwich brought to him. The treasure lasted five days, but the SS officer automatically went on ordering a sandwich for him and he survived thanks to this ingenious investment. 'I was young, very courageous, and my mind was very quick.' Then, liberated by the Americans, he returned to his native city. Father, mother, sister, uncles, house – nothing was left. The starving Poles hated the Jews. He escaped into Hungary, and that was the beginning of a long saga of misery, despair, and international organisations, all of which led him to Australia. A feminine hand touches my arm.

'The plane is about to take off; I'll take you to your seat.'

'Good luck!' says the man.

We have taken off now, and I can hear his voice to my left, on the other side of the aisle.

'I'm sitting here right next to you, if you need anything.' During the four-hour trip he doesn't say another word. I'm afraid he feels embarrassed about having revealed so much. I had already noticed this phenomenon at the hospital. People would come in, friends and strangers alike, sit down and disclose themselves without the slightest warning. This behavior, quite new to me, occurred so often that I questioned Dr T. 'Why do you think Dr Freud sat behind the couch?' he said. I am the ideal garbage can, since I can't look. Ideal because looking is judging. They confide their burdens, never their joys. My anonymous quality reassures them. My blindness is the darkness and the grille of the confessional. Most of them avoid me if we happen to meet later on.

Among these people who intrude into my life, there are several types:

– the pest, who can't conceive of my not being at the total disposition of everyone. He sits down, tells me about himself, his ailments, his life, his friends, whom I don't know – all this for hours. When, completely exhausted, I protest, he becomes violent because, after all, he has come all the way to entertain me! Not to accept his charity is unacceptable to him. Garbage can I am, garbage can I must remain;

– the frustrated one, who throws himself at me in an attempt to fill up a void. Out of self-interest, he wants to please me by arranging my things, which enrages me. Exasperated, I am forced to mark out my territory in order not to be dispossessed;

– finally, a more amusing variety, who takes advantage of the situation to live out a fantasy. Six months ago, on the plane between Bangkok and Singapore, a Scotsman offered me some champagne. I accepted gratefully and he told me about Glasgow, his hometown, his school, his clan, his rugby team, in a heavy Scottish accent and with much emotion. With the help of the champagne, he even got around to the beautiful Highland red-heads. When he got off the plane, I said to the hostess: 'I have actually met a generous Scotsman.'

'What Scotsman?'

'My neighbor.'

'But . . . he was Chinese.'

Singapore: thousands of stories of boutiques, restaurants, hotel rooms. Caved-in sidewalks. Singapore. A young Indian woman lends me her thin and somewhat hairy arm, Englishmen jostle me, Chinese stamp my passport. It's curious to notice that neither in Tokyo, where I stopped over for a few hours on my way from New York, nor in Bangkok, nor in Denpasar, nor even in very bureaucratic Singapore, did any customs official show the least surprise at my eyes looking out at him from the passport photo. Nor was there any reaction to the words 'Distinguishing marks: none.' Asian tact?

On a telephone I dial several numbers; they ring but no one answers. It's Sunday. My last hope is Rose, a young Chinese woman whom I met two months ago on a beach of the Island. I hardly know her, but she answers. Her voice is precise and shows no emotion or surprise.

'Don't move. I'll be there in twenty minutes.'

'Why don't you just give me your address?'

'No, I'll be there in twenty minutes.' She hangs up.

I have only one small bag with me, so I don't have to wait for my luggage. Everything goes very smoothly. I can't repeat this too often: blind people should know that it is easier to travel than to stay at home. The only obstacles are psychological and financial, which can be quite sufficient.

Precisely twenty minutes later, Rose's presence is heralded by a subtle perfume and I feel my arm being taken and my nose overpowered. Getting into the car, I almost fall flat on my face. The floorboard and the seat are much higher than normal. Is it a Toyota jeep? A minibus? No, my hand touches leather and satiny smooth chrome.

'It's a Rolls-Royce, a Silver Cloud, which matches your glasses.' She laughs. 'It's my father's, but he is in Europe. He has eleven cars, but I don't have one anymore. It costs too much to keep them up.'

Oh, Singapore! I can hear Aho's voice saying, 'A Rolls-Royce is very good!'

'I am broke,' Rose continues. 'Lousy business deals, a lousy guy, and gambling.'

'Are you married?'

'That's the lousy guy. A gangster, a real one. I like gangsters.' Eternal China, Confucius, help us! She lives with her parents, and that's where we're going to have dinner.

'How do you do, young man,' says Madam Chu. 'Please excuse me, but I don't have time to dine with you.'

Other Chinese women shake my hand. I hear the rapid clicking of mah-jong counters as a spicy soup is served.

'They have been playing since this morning,' Rose informs me in her caustic voice.

'For money?'

'Naturally!'

I can almost see the way she shrugs her shoulders. From a nearby kitchen come the sounds of pots and pans clanking together and the shrill voices of Malaysian women. I sense a sort of communal life, which is never found in a Western household, especially not in one as opulent as this. The mah-jong, the cooking, the dinner, and Rose's younger sister, Pauline, who is trying on a dress for the approaching Chinese New Year – it blends together to the accompaniment of general conversation. The phone rings. It's Father. Madam Chu calls out:

'Rose! Your father wants to talk to you.'

Rose comes back.

'Gold has gone up. He's afraid I'll sell too late and miss the profit. I manage his gold as well as other clients'. I don't think they have confidence in me anymore. Two years ago, I made a lot of money, more than two million dollars, but I lost it all. Gambling and that gangster got me into some bad deals, and I wasn't following the market closely enough. Now I go to the office at night, from ten to three. That way, I keep away from gambling and gangsters.' She laughs. There is no happiness in it, but there's no self-pity, either. 'I like poor people,' she says finally.

On the way to her office, Rose drops me off at Ronnie's. He's a friend who, having just got back from Malaysia, has finally answered my phone call. Ronnie is a Rumanian diamond merchant whose family has been in Singapore for three generations. During daytime hours, he devotes himself to the very lucrative diamond business; at night he is explosively transformed into some Ubu-like character, dressed in Chinese robes, with phosphorescent hooks used to fish at night anchored in the silk. He appears when least expected on a makeshift stage erected for a single night, for one week, or for however long the temple feast may last. With his Nikon he shoots close-ups of the Chinese opera singers' heavily plastered faces. They all know him and no longer pay any attention to him. From time to time, the dancing king of the monkeys gives him a sharp rap with his bamboo cane, just for fun. All of them like and respect him. They have understood that Ronnie is trying to capture a disappearing Singapore gradually swallowed up by the concrete towers Rose's father is building.

His apartment is crowded with a multitude of gods and altars, as well as two cats, a Malaysian transvestite, a French lady traveler, and a Japanese masseur whose name sounds like Macchabée, the French slang for corpse. All these people sleep on mats and mattresses scattered in the various rooms, but I have a room to myself. Ronnie and I go out right away and a few minutes later, totally deafened by cymbals and gongs, I find myself sitting in the wings of an open-air theater. The din of a

Mongolian horde reverberates against the concrete walls of
the high-rise buildings that surround us. Out of modesty, the
actresses change inside huge jute sacks. Ronnie tells them that
if they need any help, they shouldn't hesitate to ask me. I'm
ideal for the job of dresser. Before I know it, they have made
me an integral part of the company. Between performances,
they make me sit on the Emperor's throne holding an enormous
opera fan – a rather intriguing character. We talk for hours over
tiny cups of green tea, which sets the nerves on edge and makes
sleep impossible. In front of the stage the neighbourhood people
gather. A child asks me, 'Are you a wise man?' An old man
smokes little pipefuls of opium. One of the actors tells me
confidentially that he prefers heroin. He uses the American word
smack; behind the sets tradition seems to have cracks in it.

They all share a passion for this profession that barely provides
them with a living. This government of bankers and promoters
doesn't care what will happen to them. Everything around them
flourishes while they are dying. But nothing can tear them
away from this thousand-year-old drama. The costumes are
magnificent; they make me touch them with my fingers. The
sets are worth thousands of dollars: silk tapestries embroidered
with gold thread, some of which were brought long, long ago
from the great Mother Country, China.

I try out the musical instruments. A woman hands me a soft
object with two strings and slips a ring over my fingers. I finally
realise that it's a drink: Seven-Up poured into a plastic bag, with
a straw sticking out.

I sense the huge buildings and their overpowering mass,
their menacing weight towering over the fragile stage that has
survived for more than three thousand years. Between these
concrete walls, the roar of the Princess, the bellowing of the
war lord, the commands of the Emperor have a strangely
anachronistic echo, yet an immortal sound. Ronnie is furiously
taking pictures in a never-ending race against time. Every day
another part of the old Singapore dies. At dawn, bulldozers level
a temple. Alerted by his network of informers, Ronnie wakes
up and goes to photograph.

A medium is in a trance at the Temple of the Two Brothers,

near the river. It is full moon. I touch the sampans slowly rocked by the water and get splinters in my fingers. It's the wood of Noah's Ark.

'I belong to the Temple Committee,' Ronnie tells me. 'You can ask the medium for a divination.'

Since the cabalistic fortuneteller in New York, I have a certain disdain for this kind of activity, but curiosity gets the better of me. In front of an altar, sitting cross-legged in a large ebony armchair with intertwined dragons above his head, the medium is motionless. An excessively long tongue is hanging out of his mouth and his eyes are closed. I make a small donation and kneel on a little cushion in front of the armchair. Showing only the whites of his eyes, he speaks and the interpreter translates:

'You think too much. It's useless and only tires the head. You want to leave and wonder if you ought not to go home. For the time being you mustn't go back to London. You must stay here.'

Out of a habit acquired in colonial times, he uses London to mean the home of any white man, and his reference to Singapore includes the whole Far East. It is perfectly true that since being cut off from reading, I am unable to slow down my brain and I think too much. What am I looking for at this end of the world? I don't know, but the fact is that my heart is lighter here.

I think too much and my brain has cramps, to such a point that it succumbs to a sort of catatonic state. Nervous tension radiates from every hair on my head, and insomnia haunts my nights.

'You must meet Rama,' Ronnie says. 'He's a neurologist who practices in Singapore.'

I have heard of him. Three years ago, I read an article by him on the way certain Hindu sects control pain. Later, after a sleepless night, I go to see Rama. As usual when I meet somebody for the first time, all my senses except of course my sight become hyperactive. What strikes me first about Rama is a smell.

'You have just been operating?'

'Yes, for eight hours. How can you tell?'

'The smell of the operating room.'

'But I showered twice, shaved, and put on cologne.'

In the ensuing hours, as our conversation proceeds, the chemical smell is replaced by a sweetish one, Rama's own.

'We still don't know much. There's a whole assortment of sophisticated procedures that involve stimulating the visual cortex directly with a series of electrodes connected to a tiny television camera and thus getting luminous dots. The idea was to make a helmet or hat that would contain the camera, which could be hooked up to direct contacts in the visual cortex made through the skull. All we were trying to do was to allow a blind person who still has his cortex and visual memory to be able to cross the street and make out obstacles with the help of these luminous signals. No possibility of recognising a building or a face. Between the moment your retina registers what you see and the moment your brain finally sees it, an enormous number of processes take place. The eye itself is already programmed, and this programme is not in the brain. The notion of left and right, for example, is coded in the eye. This notion will not make its way to the brain. The same goes for up and down. One of the difficulties with computers is similar. A computer might say, "This line is of such and such a length," without being able to say whether it is horizontal or vertical. It took a long time to solve the problem. No one will ever be able to see by impulses on the brain.'

These Frankensteinian experiments disgust me and make me feel slightly nauseated.

'What about dreams?'

'Yes, they are visual, but nobody knows what provokes them. It seems that our brain has two parts. One is concerned with only rational functions – figures, calculations, the common linguistic symbols that make it possible to communicate with others; and then there's another part of the brain which is more emotional and functions entirely out of appreciation of values and judgments. We are seldom aware of this part except in an "artistic" situation. You listen to music or look at a painting and you form an opinion; you feel happy, sad, disgusted, but you can't really say why. And all art critics and their evaluations are a lot of rubbish. They are trying to apply rational values to a system they don't apply to.'

'Like theology?'

'Yes, that's right. It's the same kind of bullshit. With the help of imprinted contact lenses, you can visually stimulate either the rational or the nonrational part of your brain. Take an old lady with a split brain – let's say her brain was divided in half in an operation. You transmit a pornographic image to the dominant, rational part. You ask her to describe it. She answers, "It's a young woman copulating with a dog." And that's all she'll say. Now you transmit the image to the dominated, nonrational, emotional part, and she'll get angry, her blood pressure will go up; she'll turn red, but won't be able to tell you what it is.'

'Is that because she's censoring herself?'

'No, she simply can't tell you what it is. And now, if you take the old lady, all of her, and connect the two sides of her brain, she will know immediately that it's the picture of a young woman having sex with a dog. She'll get angry with you and say, "Look here, you disgusting man, take that away immediately or I'll call the police!" That's how the brain works.'

The tension built up in Rama by eight hours of operating is beginning to disappear. I listen to him but don't know quite what to do with the information he is providing me, which gets funnier as he goes along.

Night has fallen. Thousands of crickets are singing over the rhythmic bassoon of the toads. The noise of the city rises from the bottom of the hill.

'To get back to your case, if we were in the West I would suggest Valium because you must relax your brain. Since we are in Asia, I would suggest opium.'

'Opium,' Rama said. We retreat this evening to a colonial house on the top of a hill at the edge of Singapore's last jungle. A businessman lives there, but he is different from the ones with offices on Orchard Boulevard. Mr Chang is there, too, with his attaché case containing a pipe and several balls of opium. He could be hanged for this, and we wouldn't fare much better. But nobody is thinking about that. Throughout the night Mr Chang attends to the pipe. It has been seven years since I last smoked opium.

Seven-year-old images come back in waves. How different then was Asia, and I. There was the foul, stinking cancer of Vietnam. I see the eyes of those three thousand orphans herded together in Saigon, hanging onto my legs to prevent me from leaving, so that I would stay and play with them. A five-year-old boy laughs as he limps along on his crutch, swinging his tiny stump. A little girl, without arms, ashamed, stands off at a distance. And there is that little eight-year-old girl found one morning on the steps of the orphanage, her skin transparent. With her arms outstretched as if on a cross, she is letting herself die. She is the only crucifix I have ever seen. A grandmother who has gone mad, chained to a heavy table, watches the life go out of the child, and bursts into laughter at regular intervals. In the street, gangs of children throw rocks at anything that looks American. I focus on the dying eyes and the translucent face of the little girl. Of all the images of this war that I carry around inside, that's the one that the opium forces upon me tonight.

Laos was not too contaminated then; life was still gentle. At Luang Prabang, along the river shore, a debonair old king would play bridge and watch gilded, dragon-covered barges glide before him. Saturday night, a grenade exploded in a cinema, killing eighteen people, but I was told that it was some man blowing himself up out of despair over a lost love. He didn't want to die alone. But in the jungle the cancer nibbles away. The Pathet Lao is advancing silently, in Ho Chi Minh sandals made out of old tires. In the enchanted pagodas of the royal capital, incense gently rises before my eyes. Oh, yes, Asia and I have definitely both changed.

I smoked my first opium pipe in the mountains of the Northeast, in a Meo village. I arrived on an evening of dramatic sunset, like a bleeding echo of what was happening far beyond the mountains. The Meos were fleeing the Plain of Jars and advancing along the crests. Exhausted, moving from one charred field to another and trying to plant sickly rice and forbidden poppies, they had arrived at the end of the road, the border of China and Thailand. At the end of the road, there was a camp of listless refugees dying by the hundreds from typhus or malaria.

*   *   *

Mr Chang, a gutsy little man, goes on rolling opium as he tells the story of the arrival of the Japanese in Singapore. Captured, he was sent as a prisoner to Burma to work on building railroad tracks 'out there near the bridge on the River Kwai,' he says with a laugh. But he jumped off the train, crossed over into Thailand, and disappeared into the Golden Triangle. He tells all this calmly, with little chuckles and his own very special sense of humor. He showed up again some years later after setting up a business, the only kind possible besides jade: opium. 'I can say that at least once in my life I had a lot of money.' He falls silent and becomes thoughtful. We all turn to our thoughts.

A cockatoo laughs in the last jungle of Singapore. Opium has brought about the desired effect. The tension created by being deprived of the help and the pleasure of images has disappeared. The drug helps relax my lobes and my thoughts.

It was for a similar reason that I smoked my first pipe. I had swum in ice-cold water and my whole back was hit by what seemed to be excessively painful shingles. I asked my Meo host to give me a massage, and he did it very well with two of his sons – so well that he made me scream with pain. After two hours of this treatment, I could walk without too much discomfort. 'We'll have to do it again tomorrow, unless you smoke.'

'He doesn't mean Marlboros,' said my interpreter; 'he means opium.' For the Meos, poppies are the only medicine. Opium is pleasure, but it is also a remedy.

A few days after that, Rama comes to see me.

'Let's go dancing! I want you to meet Benita, a very beautiful Tamil. She has come down with an incurable disease, and in a few weeks she'll be blind. She can't get used to the idea. She's getting bitter and depressed. I'd like you to talk to her.'

I think of that blind New York writer whom I had wanted to meet when I got out of the hospital in order to ask him for such technical information as how much he used Braille or cassette tapes, just to take advantage of his experience and gain some time. He answered the person who conveyed my request to him, 'I have nothing to do with those people,' meaning the blind. My messenger was scandalised, but I wasn't. I understood that ugly reaction perfectly well, but I was annoyed to lose a source of information that could have been precious to me. Later, in fact, I did succeed in meeting him.

We meet Rose and two of her sisters with their husbands or fiancés at the Club, which seems to be the 'in' place for successful people. We have picked up Benita on the way. She is petite and has long, obviously black hair. 'I'm rather pretty,' she says, but without vanity, and she adds, ironically, 'What people like most are my eyes.' She talks while dancing, without any abandon, totally unrelaxed. Her voice is somewhat harsh, but above all terribly preoccupied. 'I still have good peripheral vision, but my central vision has disappeared. I had to quit my job because it had become a web of lies. I'm a language teacher. No one at school was aware of my problem. For a year I pretended that I could still read. I would lock myself in my office so that nobody could enter and discover me correcting a paper by holding it an inch from my eyes. I was going crazy. I broke up with the boyfriend I had been living with for two years. Sentimental relationships aren't enough for me anymore; I need something else, spiritual support. But up to now I haven't found anything; I feel useless and full of self-pity. I can't accept what is happening to me, even though I have known since childhood that it would happen. When I was fifteen, my parents tried to marry me off in a hurry, without saying anything to my prospective in-laws or to my fiancé. I escaped and have been living like a Westerner, which has been a shock for my parents. You must understand that, among Asians, abnormal or handicapped children are a cause for shame. They are hidden away, no one talks about them, excuses are invented – an accident, for instance. It must absolutely not be a birth defect.'

I listen to Benita, and as she talks, she gradually relaxes. She's a girl who has character and quality. She'll manage much better than others. But she is proud, independent, and demanding. She is going to suffer. I tell her:

'You've got to realise that this time you won't be able to manage all by yourself and that you will need other people's love to support you.'

'Phooey! Love! No, I'm thinking of something else. Have you

heard about a spiritual breathing technique that lets you be born again? You go back to the fetal stage and by doing so give birth to yourself.'

'Yes, I know some people here in Singapore who practice it. Why not? There isn't only one solution. That one isn't mine for the time being, but it may be yours.'

There are a lot of people on the dance floor. Regardless, I dance to some rock-and-roll music with a wild Japanese girl. Rama is beginning to get seriously drunk.

'I'd like a magic recipe that would allow me to relax, but I'm a surgeon, nothing but a surgeon. My hands guide me, direct me. People tell me, "Find a hobby, fixing things around the house, gardening, anything that will keep your hands occupied." I might as well stir my drink with my prick! While I sleep, I rehearse the operation I have to perform next or go over the one I have just finished, especially when there's been an accident, a death. Guilt! Even when I have nothing to blame myself for. I remember that woman who told me, "How I love the smell of the earth just after the rain!" She died on the operating table. Fuck! Every time it rains, the smell of damp earth makes this goddam feeling of guilt rise up in me. So I drink. I'm a surgeon, nothing but a surgeon. I don't give a damn about being the good guy or the bad guy. I come from a Brahman family in southern Madras. You must come with me. I'll introduce you to my nieces, magnificent girls who are open to the cosmos.'

Drunk, Rama starts reciting Tamil poetry and sayings. 'If you can't die at the front, die in the cunt.'

Rose has left for her office, to keep an eye on the palpitations of gold. I dance with a tall Chinese woman who kisses me on the mouth and tells me that her husband is very jealous and that she has never been unfaithful to him. Armed with this information, I take her politely back to the table. I hear Benita's laughter, which makes me feel happy.

'I knew she had to see you.'

I think I understand what Rama means, and I feel a little less useless.

THIRTY-TWO

The palm grove echoes with the song of thousands of birds. The monsoon has moved on. The sun is still cool, and on the beach, behind the frangipani hedge, the languid sea whispers. The fishermen of Sakenan Island shout long calls to one other from the coral reef, and a woman sings as she tosses offerings into the waves. I got back from Singapore last night with my new visa in my pocket and now I surrender to the scent of the flowers, to the silence enhanced by the songs of the birds and to the sun evaporating the dew. Singapore, the whiskey, bars, girls, cymbals, and Chinese operas gradually fade away. Water floods the island. In the *sawas*, the rice has already been planted; there will be a good harvest. There haven't been such fine rains for two years. Secretive flowers grow overnight.

January. How far away New York is with its snowstorms and those long hours spent listening to the wind blowing against the window. How far away Valushka is. Valushka . . . how far. I don't hear the birds' song anymore, the flowers close their petals. Valushka is a forbidden city to me, a thought that pierces my heart with an unexpected stab. She invades my night and unites me with her and rocks me in the billows. I feel like kissing the mouths of volcanoes. How is it that my memory cannot forget this face I have never seen? And when I see you in my dreams, with your dark eyes and their questioning look, asking that question I wasn't able to answer, when I see this face in my dreams, with its Russian cheekbones and slightly turned-up nose framed by Venetian hair, I know that I see you better than if I really saw you. I don't know what my own face looks like anymore. If I want to imagine it, I have to think of a photo – the one on my passport, for example. But recalling my image directly is impossible. Sometimes, while brushing my teeth, I look fixedly at the mirror in which I know I am reflected. No answer to my questioning. I believe that from a certain age on, your face carries your signature, and it is a great disappointment not to see what is inscribed on mine.

For eight months now, the Island has been working on my body and my soul. I won't entirely realise this until I leave the magic circle that surrounds it. There's an old woman who always comes when least expected to give me a massage, as if called by some secret signal. She rubs me with clay, oil, salves she makes herself. Her fingers pinch, detaching the muscles along my ribs, shoulders, and thighs. She tells stories, and her laughter is young, like her hands and her strength. But little by little, she falls silent and a kind of torpor descends on me. I am as naked as a worm in the hands of this old woman burned by the sun and the salt. Old guardian of bodies' youth. She cracks her knuckles on my forehead, and the sound of the bones resounds within my skull. It is death that is massaging me, that I know. She massages me as one would prepare for a feast – her feast. She puts my hand on her thigh to stretch my fingers. Her thigh is full, firm. She farts quietly. She is certainly alive.

'Suda Tuan, it's over.'

She argues about the fee and asks me to lend her five thousand rupees. I refuse, but she doesn't get upset. You don't lose anything by trying. I hear her discreetly stealing a few clove-flavoured cigarettes. No, not stealing, there is a tacit agreement between us, but she's not quite aware of it.

And then there's the massage of the soul, the long hours of silence, of solitude. Long hours beginning at the end of the afternoon, when the sun has gone down and even the birds stop singing. Night is not only darkness, but also sounds that carry different vibrations, air that seems denser, as if laden with spirits. My thoughts have been massaged again and again by these hours. The panic I felt during the first days, when I was dreaming that some hope would surge from the emptiness of the night, has totally disappeared. These hours of silence, poetry, and reflection are now part of my being. A useless life, a selfish life. I will die without children, without having given anything to the world except for some insignificant paintings and films. But life under the volcanoes rephrases the questions and relieves their intensity. And the eternal, endlessly renewed lament of the sea beneath my window anesthetises me.

I go into town anyway, to the school for blind children, to offer mobility courses, to talk to them. The directress is interested; she has no money, and I'm a volunteer. Language classes, piano lessons, I protest, 'But I don't know how to play!' She doesn't believe me. There are forty-seven blind children; the directress makes them sing in chorus. They are well disciplined; they laugh. I play them a little piece by Bach, the only music I still have in my fingertips. Not enough money, not enough instructors. They are taught basket weaving, repairing chairs – the blind person's trade. In Europe, it took the disappearance of rush-seated chairs everywhere, even in churches, to banish the stereotype of the blind man on the sidewalk mending chairs in the middle of a circle of kids. I feel weary and, once again, nauseated. What can I give them? What do I want to give them? This desire to vomit is not a very good sign. It's not their sadness but their laughter that breaks my heart.

When I'm confronted with my tribe, in the reservation that has been assigned to us, I can't hold back this feeling of disgust in my stomach. I'm afraid, like the black who has made it in the outside world and walks back through the ghetto. The ghetto will always concern us, him and me.

The rains have gone away; now the Island under the sun smokes as if it were a cauldron. The birds have begun singing again, louder than ever, and Kayan goes out to sea in the chill of the early morning. Yesterday, we caught a young shark.

'Feel it! Feel it!' he says, excitedly.

He laughs because I can't guess what kind of fish it is. I hold it by the base of the tail, as round as the body of a conger eel. A moray? No. I feel the muscular fish twisting in my hand and then, suddenly, I know that it is dead. An abandonment that one cannot mistake. I tell Kayan:

'It's dead.'

'Oh, no! It takes a long time for it to die.' He takes the fish by the tail and sees that it is indeed dead. 'I must have damaged one of its vital organs with the harpoon.'

We are far beyond the reef. No breeze disturbs the air and, in spite of the distance, I hear the sounds from the shore. The three volcanoes to the east have punctured their cocoon of mist and clouds, and behind us, beyond the horizon, the volcano of Lombok, immense, improbable, mythical, surges up from the sea. Softly, simply, Kayan describes, and I imagine, with the help of my memories. But the more I imagine, the more I am aware of my failure. I manage to picture in my mind the three volcanoes with their feet in the rice paddies, the white coastline that becomes black where streams of lava flowed into the sea. But I realise I am cut off from whatever it is that makes this morning unique in the history of the universe, from the singularity of this fleeting revelation of one instant of infinity. It's as if one were to describe a face but not the expression on it.

However, little by little, I hear in Kayan's voice a kind of distant music, which contains the menace of the volcanoes, the infinity of the sea, the mystery of the horizon, and in all of that the fragility of the *jukung* and of us in it. And when his voice falls silent, I hear in the silence how eternal everything seems to be around us, we who are so transitory. And the volcanoes, piercing through the clouds, contemplate us with the ironic regard one has for the short-lived. A spear of thunder assails the male volcano and bounds off again into the sun. Deep within the temples, pythons uncoil their crystal scales. Perhaps after all I will go to Makassar.

Merta Sari, 1980
Lassay, 1982

JANICE ELLIOTT

THE ITALIAN LESSON

The Castello of San Salvatore is an exclusive and enchanted holiday place set in the hills above Florence and far removed from the dangerous real world below. It is just the spot for polytechnic lecturer William Farmer to pursue his search for E. M. Forster and for his wife Fanny to get over a recent stillbirth. Just the setting, too, for some wicked observation of cultural pretensions and a host of kindly but wildly funny creations.

Janice Elliott manipulates her characters and her plot with a masterly and light touch. THE ITALIAN LESSON is a wry and clever novel about the British abroad, at once a modern reworking of Forster's themes and, at the same time, strikingly original.

'There is no doubt in my mind that she is one of the most resourceful and imaginative living English novelists'
Paul Bailey in the London Standard

'Janice Elliott has written an elegant comedy that conceals on every page an unexploded bomb of disaster. Her interlocking events seem at first both sunny and funny – yet below the surface lurks pain and revelation. A memorable book that lingers on'
David Hughes in the Mail on Sunday

NIGEL HAMILTON

MONTY
Volume 3
THE FIELD-MARSHAL

*The award-winning biography of the victor of the Battle of
Alamein, of D-Day and of Normandy*

MONTY:
The Field-Marshal 1944–1976

'. . . well balanced, well planned and well written, put
together on a basis of enormous research meticulously and
critically conducted . . . gives a fresh account of one of the
outstanding, most significant and most complicated men of our
time'

Sir John Hackett

'There can never be a definitive life of anyone, but these three
volumes come as near to that achievement as possible. It is
safe to say that they are most unlikely to be superseded in the
foreseeable future . . . An indispensable work of reference
. . . Nelson was a great man and so was Monty. He deserves a
great biography and he has got it'

Lord Blake in the Financial Times

MONTY: THE FIELD-MARSHAL 1944–1976 is the third of
three volumes, all of which are published by Sceptre.

WINSTON S. CHURCHILL

THE RIVER WAR

In 1881 the Mahdi's rebellion plunged the Sudan into bloodshed and confusion. Egyptian armies sent to recover the territory were routed and destroyed. All outside control and administration had been wiped out. Mr Gladstone's Government decided that British interests in the area were to be withdrawn. General Gordon was sent to Khartoum to bring out the surviving officials, soldiers and Egyptian subjects. But, as the Mahdi's forces surrounded Khartoum, Gordon was trapped and doomed.

THE RIVER WAR tells of the expedition of reconquest that, under General Kitchener, fought its way up the Nile. The young Winston Churchill was there. This is his classic account of the expedition and the final Battle of Omdurman.

sceptre

JOHN COLVILLE

THE FRINGES OF POWER
Downing Street Diaries
Volume Two: 1941–April 1955

With new material never before published

The Diaries of Sir John Colville, Private Secretary to Chamberlain, Churchill, Attlee, and Princess Elizabeth are vital and enthralling historical documents.

JANUARY 23, 1945 The P.M. (Churchill) said to me, 'Make no mistake, all the Balkans except Greece, are going to be Bolshevised; and there is nothing I can do to prevent it. There is nothing I can do for poor Poland either.'

'The best picture we have of Churchill from below . . . Churchill's humanity glows on these pages'
John Vincent in the Sunday Times

'Marvellously credible . . . he domesticates the legendary, without trivialising it – a great literary achievement'
Peregrine Worsthorne in the Sunday Telegraph

VOLUME ONE: 1939–OCTOBER 1941 is also published by Sceptre.

ALLAN MASSIE

AUGUSTUS

AUGUSTUS reconstructs the lost memoirs of Augustus, true founder of the Roman Empire, son of Julius Caesar, friend and later foe of Mark Antony, patron of Horace and Virgil. Massie has breathed conviction and realism into one of the greatest periods of the past, creating an unforgettable array of characters and incidents.

'All the drama of Graves's *I, Claudius* with an added mordant humour'
Harriet Waugh in the Spectator

'He makes Augustus credible as a man: wily, ruthless, shrewd, generous, admirable'
Andrew Sinclair in The Times

'A private and public history that never loses its pace or grip. Massie summons up a Roman scene that frankly exists as much in the late twentieth century as in the first century B.C.'
Boyd Tonkin in The Listener

'A great achievement by any standard'
The Scotsman

'A marvellous historical novel, written with style and verve . . . ranks with Robert Graves's classic *I, Claudius* and *Claudius The God*. All the colour, cruelty and splendour of a great pagan civilisation are given their due by a novelist at the height of his powers'
Dublin Sunday Press

sceptre

Current and forthcoming titles from Sceptre

JANICE ELLIOTT

THE ITALIAN LESSON

NIGEL HAMILTON

MONTY:
The Field-Marshal 1944–1976

WINSTON S. CHURCHILL

THE RIVER WAR

JOHN COLVILLE

THE FRINGES OF POWER
Volume Two: 1941–April 1955

ALAN MASSIE

AUGUSTUS

BOOKS OF DISTINCTION